A WAKE-UP CALL TO SAFEGUARD OUR PLANET'S FUTURE

STOP DESTROYING EARTH

OSMAN KARAKAS

About Book

Book Title: **STOP DESTROYING EARTH:**

A WAKE-UP CALL TO SAFEGUARD OUR PLANET'S FUTURE

Type: Digital E-Book

Format: **PDF**

Size: 6X9 inches - 15.24X22.89 cm

Total Pages: **386**

E-mail: okarakas@hotmail.com

Web: www.osmankarakas.com

CONTENTS

Preface

Welcome to "Stop Destroying Earth: A Wake-Up Call to Safeguard Our Planet's Future." In the pages that follow, we embark on a journey to explore the critical environmental challenges facing our planet and the urgent need for collective action to address them.

Our world is at a crossroads. The impacts of climate change, the loss of biodiversity, the specter of pandemics, and the looming possibility of conflicts over resources all underscore the fragility of the Earth's ecosystems. We are witnessing the consequences of our unsustainable practices and our failure to live in harmony with the natural world.

This book is a call to action, a plea for awareness, and a source of hope. It is a comprehensive exploration of the complex web of issues that threaten our planet's future. From the Extinction Crisis and the need for population reduction strategies to the potential impacts of future viruses and the looming specter of war, we delve into the challenges that demand our attention and immediate action.

Throughout these pages, we aim to not only inform but also inspire. We believe that by understanding the gravity of these issues and recognizing our role in their creation, we can spark change. We can make choices in our daily lives that reduce our ecological footprint, advocate for policies that prioritize sustainability, and support initiatives that protect our planet's precious ecosystems.

This book is not just a collection of facts and figures; it is a call for empathy, a reminder of our responsibility to the Earth and its inhabitants. It emphasizes the moral imperative of environmental stewardship and the interconnectedness of all life on this planet. It is a plea for a more sustainable, equitable, and harmonious future.

As you embark on this journey through the pages of "Stop Destroying Earth," we invite you to reflect on your own relationship with the natural world, consider the actions you can take to make a positive difference, and join us in the urgent task of safeguarding our planet's future. Together, we can rise to the challenge and be the change that our Earth so desperately needs.

Thank you for taking this journey with us. The time to act is now, and together, we can ensure a brighter future for all living beings on our beloved planet Earth.

Osman Karakas

Chapter 1: Earth's History (As Known)

Introduction:

In the vast tapestry of the cosmos, our home planet, Earth, holds a unique and cherished place. As we embark on this journey through the annals of history, we are about to uncover the chronicles of Earth's past, a saga that predates even the earliest human civilizations. Understanding Earth's history is not a mere exercise in nostalgia; it is a powerful lens through which we can comprehend the challenges and triumphs that have shaped our world.

The significance of comprehending Earth's history lies in its undeniable connection to the current state of our planet. As inhabitants of this blue orb hurtling through space, we are bound by an intricate web of natural forces, human endeavors, and cosmic happenings. Our actions, both past and present, have left indelible marks on the landscape and the delicate balance of life. To move forward, we must first look back.

This chapter serves as a compass, pointing us toward a profound truth: that we must learn from our past to avert further destruction. Each page reveals insights into the triumphs and failures of humanity, the evolution of our planet, and the consequences of our actions. It beckons us to acknowledge the weight of history and to embrace our role as stewards of Earth's future.

As we embark on this exploration of Earth's history, let us heed the lessons of the past, for they are the keys to unlocking a future where Earth, our irreplaceable home, can flourish once more.

Setting the Stage:

Understanding Earth's History in the Context of Its Current State

The story of Earth's past is not just a collection of ancient events relegated to history books; it is the foundational narrative of our existence. It is the tale of a planet that has endured for billions of years, bearing witness to cataclysms and rebirths, to the emergence and evolution of life forms, and to the rise and fall of civilizations. Yet, the importance of comprehending Earth's history extends far beyond mere curiosity about our origins; it is a critical aspect of navigating the challenges that confront us today.

Imagine a grand theater with Earth as its stage. On this grand stage, the elements of our planet, from the restless tides to the towering mountains, have played their roles for eons. The actors in this drama include the countless species that have come and gone, each contributing to the intricate tapestry of life. And center stage, in the spotlight, is humanity—a species that, in the blink of an eye in geological terms, has transformed the stage itself.

Understanding Earth's history is akin to reading the script of this cosmic play. It provides us with context, backstory, and a sense of continuity. It allows us to see how the Earth has responded to myriad challenges over the millennia and how, in turn, our actions have influenced the unfolding narrative.

Moreover, Earth's history is the chronicle of resilience and adaptation. It is a testament to the tenacity of life and the capacity of ecosystems to recover and regenerate, even in the face of severe disruptions. It tells us that nature has its own rhythm, and when we disrupt it, consequences follow.

But why does this matter in the 21st century? Why should we delve into the annals of time to grasp the past? The answer is as urgent as it is compelling: we stand at a pivotal moment in Earth's history. Our planet is facing unprecedented challenges—climate change, biodiversity loss, resource depletion, and social inequalities among them. These issues are not isolated; they are interconnected threads woven into the fabric of Earth's history.

By understanding the mistakes and successes of our ancestors, we gain wisdom. We learn which paths led to flourishing civilizations and which led to decline. We see how the misuse of resources, the disregard for nature's limits, and the neglect of our fellow beings have consequences that echo through time. And crucially, we discover that our current actions are not just choices for today; they are shaping the narrative of tomorrow.

As we delve deeper into the chapters of this book, remember that Earth's history is not a passive tale—it is an active dialogue with the present and future. It is an urgent call to reflect on the lessons of the past and to apply them in the here and now. It is an invitation to become stewards of our planet, to recognize our interconnectedness with all life, and to script a future in which Earth's story endures, not as a tragedy, but as an epic of renewal and hope.

Highlight the importance of learning from the past to prevent further destruction.

The pages of Earth's history are filled with poignant reminders of the consequences of our actions. They speak of civilizations that soared to great heights only to crumble under the weight of their own hubris. They tell of ecosystems that thrived until they were pushed to the brink of collapse. But within these stories of struggle and resilience lies the key to our future—a future where we have the power to change the narrative.

As we gaze back in time, we encounter civilizations that once prospered by harnessing the Earth's resources without thought for the consequences. They razed forests, exhausted fertile lands, and polluted their waters, believing that nature's bounty was limitless. The echoes of their mistakes reverberate through the ages, reminding us that we too face choices today that will shape the world for generations to come.

In the ancient chronicles, we see societies torn asunder by division, hatred, and violence. The scars left behind by wars and conflicts, fueled by greed and prejudice, serve as stark warnings. They teach us that the pursuit of peace and cooperation is not just a lofty ideal; it is an imperative for the survival of humanity and the planet we call home.

Yet, Earth's history is not solely a chronicle of mistakes; it is also a testament to human ingenuity, compassion, and adaptability. It tells of civilizations that revered the Earth, lived in harmony with its rhythms, and cultivated sustainable practices. These stories illuminate the path forward, demonstrating that it is possible to coexist with nature, foster peace, and build a thriving world for all.

Learning from the past is not an exercise in dwelling on regrets; it is an act of empowerment. It equips us with the knowledge and wisdom needed to make informed decisions that steer us away from the precipice of further destruction. It offers hope that we can transcend the errors of our forebears and embark on a new course—one of stewardship, compassion, and unity.

In the chapters that follow, we will delve deeper into Earth's history, unearthing valuable insights and lessons. Each page turned is an opportunity to embrace change, to make choices that are mindful of the Earth's finite resources, and to extend a hand of cooperation rather than division. It is a call to preserve the intricate web of life that sustains us and to secure a future where Earth's story is one of regeneration and harmony.

The path to preventing further destruction begins with the knowledge gained from our planet's history. It is a path illuminated by the mistakes and triumphs of those who came before us—a path that we, as stewards of Earth's future, must tread with care and purpose. Together, we can script a narrative that celebrates our ability to learn, adapt, and thrive in harmony with the planet we share with countless generations yet to come.

Section 1: How Our Galaxy System Works

The Milky Way, our cosmic home, is a breathtaking tapestry of stars, planets, and celestial wonders. To comprehend the workings of our galaxy system, we must embark on a journey through the cosmos—a journey that begins with understanding the Milky Way's structure and functioning.

1: The Structure of the Milky Way

The Milky Way, like countless other galaxies in the universe, possesses a distinct structure that shapes its appearance and behavior. Imagine our galaxy as a colossal pinwheel, composed of billions upon billions of stars arranged in spiral arms. These spiraling arms are a defining feature of the Milky Way, each containing a multitude of stars, dust, and gas.

Within this intricate tapestry, the heart of the Milky Way houses a supermassive black hole, a gravitational behemoth with the power to influence the motion of nearby stars and celestial objects. This central black hole, though daunting, plays a vital role in maintaining the equilibrium of our galaxy.

2: Earth's Position in the Milky Way

To appreciate our place in the cosmos, we must acknowledge Earth's location within the Milky Way. Our planet resides in one of the Milky Way's spiral arms, known as the Orion Arm. While Earth is but a tiny speck in the vast expanse of our galaxy, it is precisely this insignificance that lends itself to a profound realization: that our actions on this small blue dot can have profound consequences on a cosmic scale.

Our position within the Milky Way influences our perspective of the night sky. It grants us the privilege of gazing into the heart of the galaxy and witnessing the splendor of countless stars. However, it also exposes us to the cosmic forces that shape our existence, including the radiation from distant stars and cosmic phenomena.

3: Influence of Galaxy Characteristics on Earth

The Milky Way's characteristics extend their influence far beyond the boundaries of our solar system. Our galaxy's gravitational forces, magnetic fields, and radiation patterns all have subtle yet significant impacts on Earth's conditions. These influences touch upon a range of phenomena, from the magnetic field that protects our planet from harmful solar radiation to the cosmic dust that occasionally graces our atmosphere as meteors.

Moreover, the Milky Way's position within the greater universe affects our cosmic context. It determines our interactions with neighboring galaxies, the motion of our galaxy through intergalactic space, and even the ebb and flow of cosmic materials that contribute to the formation of stars and planetary systems.

As we embark on this journey through the cosmos, it is essential to grasp the intricacies of our galaxy system. Understanding the Milky Way's structure, Earth's position within it, and the galaxy's influence on our planet's conditions is a fundamental step toward comprehending the larger narrative of Earth's history and the challenges we face in preserving our planet's future.

Section 2: The Human Toll

A historical overview of the Earth's population growth and its impact on resources.

Throughout the annals of history, the human journey has been one of astonishing growth and transformation. In this section, we embark on a voyage through time, tracing the contours of Earth's population growth and the profound consequences it has wrought upon our planet's precious resources.

1: The Early Inhabitants

The story of humanity's population growth begins with humble origins. Our distant ancestors, hunter-gatherer societies, led nomadic lives, dwelling in harmony with nature's rhythms. Their populations were sparse, and their impact on the environment was relatively minimal. It was an era where sustainability was a way of life, and resources were cherished.

2: Agricultural Revolution and Population Expansion

With the advent of agriculture, a seismic shift occurred. The Agricultural Revolution marked a pivotal moment in human history, allowing for the cultivation of crops and the domestication of animals. This agricultural surplus facilitated the growth of human populations in a way never before seen.

As societies transitioned from nomadic lifestyles to settled farming communities, population numbers surged. The surplus food led to denser populations, the formation of villages and towns, and eventually the emergence of great civilizations. The transition, however, was not without consequences. Forests were cleared, rivers dammed, and soils depleted to sustain burgeoning populations.

3: Industrial Revolution and Urbanization

The Industrial Revolution heralded another transformative phase in population growth. Advancements in technology and industry led to urbanization on an unprecedented scale. Factories, railways, and cities sprang up, drawing people away from agrarian life. As populations congregated in urban centers, resource consumption soared.

The exploitation of coal, oil, and other fossil fuels powered industrialization but also left indelible marks on the environment. Pollution fouled the air and water, while deforestation and land degradation continued apace. The Earth's natural resources faced unprecedented demands, triggering concerns about sustainability and ecological balance.

4: The Modern Era and Population Explosion

The 20th century witnessed a population explosion of staggering proportions. Advances in medicine, sanitation, and agriculture dramatically increased life expectancy and food production. The global population soared, reaching milestones that were once inconceivable.

This exponential growth, while a testament to human innovation, has ushered in complex challenges. With more mouths to feed and bodies to shelter, humanity's demands on the Earth's resources intensified. Energy consumption surged, freshwater sources dwindled, and ecosystems strained under the weight of human activity.

As we delve deeper into the annals of history, we are compelled to confront the realities of Earth's population growth. It is a narrative of innovation, progress, and prosperity, but it is also one of reckoning with the consequences of our exponential expansion. Our journey through this section unveils the intricate relationship between population dynamics and the resources that sustain us, setting the stage for profound reflections on the path ahead.

Highlighting Key Milestones in Human History and Their Effects on the Environment

1. The Agricultural Revolution

The Agricultural Revolution, which dawned around 10,000 years ago, represents a pivotal moment in human history. It marked the transition from nomadic hunter-gatherer societies to settled farming communities, profoundly impacting both human civilization and the environment.

Effects on the Environment:

- **Deforestation:** The need for arable land led to widespread deforestation, altering ecosystems and diminishing habitats for countless species.

- **Soil Degradation:** Intensive farming practices, including monoculture and overuse of soil, caused soil erosion and nutrient depletion, reducing agricultural productivity.

- **Water Management:** The development of irrigation systems affected watercourses and wetlands, altering hydrological cycles and sometimes leading to salinization of soil.

- **Biodiversity Loss:** As agricultural land expanded, diverse ecosystems were replaced by monocultures, resulting in the loss of plant and animal species.

2. **The Industrial Revolution**

The Industrial Revolution, spanning the late 18th and 19th centuries, marked a profound shift in human society. It was characterized by mechanization, urbanization, and the widespread use of fossil fuels to power industry and transportation.

Effects on the Environment:

- **Air Pollution:** The burning of coal and later oil released vast quantities of pollutants into the atmosphere, contributing to smog and respiratory problems.

- **Water Pollution:** Industrial processes discharged pollutants into rivers and water bodies, severely affecting aquatic ecosystems.

- **Deforestation and Habitat Loss:** The need for resources to fuel industry led to deforestation and the alteration of landscapes.

- **Climate Change:** The combustion of fossil fuels released greenhouse gases, contributing to global warming and climate instability.

- **Resource Depletion:** The rapid extraction of resources, including minerals and forests, strained ecosystems and depleted finite resources.

These key milestones in human history underscore the interconnectedness between human progress and environmental change. The Agricultural Revolution enabled population growth but altered ecosystems, while the Industrial Revolution ushered in unprecedented technological advancement but at the cost of environmental degradation. Understanding these historical junctures allows us to grapple with the legacies they have left behind and to chart a sustainable course for the future.

Population Growth and Its Impact on Current Challenges

As we navigate the pages of history, it becomes abundantly clear that the story of human population growth is inextricably linked to the myriad challenges we face on our planet today. The exponential expansion of the human populace has not only transformed societies and economies but has also left an indelible mark on the Earth itself. In this section, we delve into how population growth has played a pivotal role in shaping the complex challenges that confront us.

Altered Landscapes

One of the most visible impacts of population growth has been the alteration of landscapes. The need for housing, agriculture, and infrastructure has led to the conversion of natural habitats into urban areas and farmland. Vast tracts of forests have been cleared, wetlands drained, and ecosystems disrupted to accommodate the burgeoning human population. The consequences are evident in dwindling biodiversity, loss of habitat for countless species, and a disruption of the delicate balance that sustains life on Earth.

1. Resource Scarcity

The relentless growth in population has strained Earth's finite resources. Freshwater sources are becoming scarcer as demand for water for drinking, agriculture, and industry escalates. Arable land is diminishing, threatening food security for millions. The extraction of minerals, fossil fuels, and other resources to meet the needs of a growing population has led to resource depletion and environmental degradation.

This resource scarcity is not limited to just one region or aspect of life. It affects communities worldwide, and it's a challenge that demands global attention. From water scarcity in arid regions to the depletion of fisheries in our oceans, the strain on resources is palpable. Sustainable resource management and conservation efforts are essential to address this pressing issue.

2. Energy Demands and Climate Change

Population growth has been accompanied by increased energy demands, primarily met through the burning of fossil fuels. This has exacerbated climate change, as the release of greenhouse gases into the atmosphere intensifies. Rising temperatures, extreme weather events, and sea-level rise are among the consequences, with profound implications for ecosystems, agriculture, and coastal communities.

Our energy choices profoundly impact our environment and the climate. Transitioning to renewable energy sources, increasing energy efficiency, and adopting sustainable practices are critical steps in mitigating the effects of climate change. The urgency of this challenge cannot be overstated, as it affects not only our generation but also future generations.

3. Urbanization and Infrastructure Needs

The shift of populations from rural to urban areas, driven by factors like employment opportunities and improved living conditions, has led to rapid urbanization. While cities offer economic and social advantages, they also generate challenges such as increased energy consumption, pollution, waste generation, and strains on transportation and infrastructure.

Urbanization is an irreversible global trend, and the sustainability of our cities is paramount. Smart urban planning, green infrastructure, and public transportation are essential components of creating livable, eco-friendly urban environments. These solutions not only enhance the quality of life for city dwellers but also reduce the ecological footprint of our urban centers.

4. Social and Economic Inequalities

Population growth has not occurred uniformly across the globe. Disparities in population growth rates, access to resources, and economic opportunities have given rise to social and economic inequalities. These inequalities, both within and between nations, pose significant challenges related to poverty, access to healthcare, education, and basic necessities.

Addressing social and economic inequalities is not only a matter of justice but also a crucial step in building a sustainable future. By promoting equitable access to resources, education, and healthcare, we can help ensure that every individual has the opportunity to lead a dignified and prosperous life while alleviating the pressure on our planet's resources.

5. Conservation and Ecosystem Health

Preserving biodiversity and maintaining ecosystem health have become pressing concerns as population growth encroaches on natural habitats. The loss of species and ecosystems threatens the balance of nature and reduces the planet's resilience in the face of environmental changes.

Conservation efforts, habitat restoration, and sustainable land use practices are fundamental to safeguarding our planet's rich biodiversity. Ecosystems provide essential services, from pollinating our crops to purifying our water, and their health is intimately connected to our own well-being.

In essence, the challenges we grapple with today—resource scarcity, climate change, urbanization, and inequalities—have been deeply influenced by the trajectory of human population growth. To navigate these challenges successfully, it is imperative to recognize the intricate relationship between population dynamics and the environment. By fostering sustainable practices, promoting social equity, and addressing the ecological footprint of our ever-expanding population, we can strive toward a harmonious coexistence with our planet.

Section 3: Hunger and Thirst

Examine the global issues of hunger, malnutrition, and lack of access to clean water.

In this section, we turn our attention to the critical global issues of hunger, malnutrition, and the lack of access to clean water. These challenges are intertwined with population growth and have profound implications for the well-being of billions of people around the world.

1. The Global Hunger Crisis

Figure: "World Hunger Statistics"

Despite the advances in food production and distribution, hunger continues to plague our world. Millions of people, including children, suffer from chronic malnutrition and go to bed hungry every night. Understanding the root causes of this crisis and exploring potential solutions is paramount to achieving a more equitable world.

- **2020**: In 2020, an estimated 9.9% of the global population, roughly 770 million people, faced chronic undernourishment, struggling to access enough food for a healthy and active life.

- **2021**: The COVID-19 pandemic exacerbated the hunger crisis, pushing an additional 118 million people into food insecurity, according to reports from the United Nations.

- **2022**: Despite efforts to address the issue, hunger persisted, affecting millions of children and adults worldwide.

Despite the advances in food production and distribution, hunger continues to plague our world. Millions of people, including children, suffer from chronic malnutrition and go to bed hungry every night. Understanding the root causes of this crisis and exploring potential solutions is paramount to achieving a more equitable world.

Root Causes of Hunger:

Hunger is not solely a result of food scarcity but is often driven by a complex web of interconnected factors:

- **Poverty**: Poverty remains a primary contributor to hunger. People living in poverty often lack the resources to access sufficient, nutritious food.

- **Inequality**: Disparities in income and access to resources exacerbate hunger. Vulnerable communities, including marginalized groups, are disproportionately affected.

- **Conflict and Instability**: Regions plagued by conflict and political instability face heightened food insecurity, as disruptions to agriculture and food distribution systems are common.

- **Climate Change**: The impact of climate change on food production, through phenomena like droughts and extreme weather events, further compounds the hunger crisis.

- **Lack of Infrastructure**: Inadequate infrastructure in some regions hinders the storage and distribution of food, leading to wastage and scarcity.

Exploring Potential Solutions:

Addressing the global hunger crisis requires a multifaceted approach:

- **Food Security Programs**: Governments and international organizations must implement food security programs that provide immediate relief to those in need.

- **Poverty Alleviation**: Tackling hunger necessitates poverty alleviation efforts, including access to education, healthcare, and employment opportunities.

- **Agricultural Innovation**: Promoting sustainable farming practices, crop diversification, and improved irrigation methods can boost food production.

- **Climate Resilience**: Developing climate-resilient agricultural systems and addressing the root causes of climate change are vital.

- **Political Stability**: Efforts to resolve conflicts and establish political stability can help alleviate hunger in regions affected by violence and instability.

Understanding the evolving figures and the underlying causes of the global hunger crisis is essential for creating effective strategies to combat this ongoing challenge. As we look to the future, it is crucial to work collectively to ensure that everyone has access to the nourishment they need for a healthy and fulfilling life.

2. Malnutrition and Its Consequences

Figure: "Effects of Malnutrition on Health"

Malnutrition extends beyond the absence of food; it encompasses inadequate access to essential nutrients. Malnourished individuals, particularly children, face lifelong health and developmental challenges. Examining the consequences of malnutrition sheds light on the urgency of addressing this issue.

- **2020**: In 2020, it was estimated that approximately 149 million children under the age of five were stunted, a condition caused by chronic malnutrition that leads to impaired growth and development.

- **2021**: The COVID-19 pandemic worsened malnutrition rates, with disruptions to food systems and healthcare services. Millions of children faced increased risk.

- **2022**: Despite efforts to combat malnutrition, it remained a significant global health challenge, affecting individuals across all age groups.

Malnutrition extends beyond the absence of food; it encompasses inadequate access to essential nutrients. Malnourished individuals, particularly children, face lifelong health and developmental challenges. Examining the consequences of malnutrition sheds light on the urgency of addressing this issue.

Consequences of Malnutrition:

Malnutrition has far-reaching effects on health and well-being:

- **Stunted Growth**: Chronic malnutrition during early childhood can lead to stunted growth, reducing a child's physical and cognitive development potential.

- **Underweight**: Malnourished children often weigh less than they should for their age, making them vulnerable to illnesses and infections.

- **Micronutrient Deficiencies**: Lack of essential vitamins and minerals can weaken the immune system and lead to conditions like anemia and night blindness.

- **Developmental Delays**: Malnutrition hinders cognitive development, impacting a child's ability to learn and thrive.

- **Increased Mortality**: Severe acute malnutrition is a leading cause of death among children under five, particularly in low-income regions.

- **Long-term Health Issues**: Malnourished children may experience long-term health problems that persist into adulthood, including a higher risk of chronic diseases.

Addressing Malnutrition:

Addressing malnutrition requires a comprehensive approach:

- **Nutritional Interventions**: Providing access to nutrient-rich foods, supplements, and fortified products can help combat malnutrition.

- **Maternal and Child Health**: Ensuring proper maternal nutrition and breastfeeding practices are vital for child nutrition.

- **Healthcare Access**: Improving access to healthcare services, particularly in underserved regions, can prevent and treat malnutrition.

- **Public Awareness**: Raising awareness about the importance of balanced diets and proper nutrition is essential for preventing malnutrition.

- **Policy and Advocacy**: Governments and organizations must advocate for policies that prioritize nutrition and support vulnerable populations.

Understanding the yearly figures and the dire consequences of malnutrition underscores the urgency of addressing this global health challenge. By taking concerted action, we can work toward a world where every individual, especially children, has the opportunity to lead a healthy and prosperous life.

3. The Quest for Clean Water

Figure: "Access to Clean Water Worldwide"

Access to clean and safe drinking water is a fundamental human right. However, a significant portion of the global population still lacks access to clean water sources. The consequences of this scarcity are far-reaching, affecting health, sanitation, and overall quality of life.

- **2020**: In 2020, it was estimated that approximately 785 million people worldwide lacked access to basic drinking water services, often relying on unsafe sources or traveling long distances to fetch water.

- **2021**: The COVID-19 pandemic highlighted the critical importance of clean water for handwashing and sanitation. Efforts were made to improve water access in vulnerable communities.

- **2022**: Despite progress, millions still faced water scarcity and waterborne diseases due to inadequate access to clean water sources.

Access to clean and safe drinking water is a fundamental human right. However, a significant portion of the global population still lacks access to clean water sources. The consequences of this scarcity are far-reaching, affecting health, sanitation, and overall quality of life.

Consequences of Water Scarcity:

Water scarcity has profound implications for communities and individuals:

- **Health Impacts**: Lack of access to clean water leads to waterborne diseases, including diarrhea, cholera, and typhoid, which can be deadly, particularly for children.

- **Sanitation Challenges**: Inadequate water supply hinders proper sanitation and hygiene practices, increasing the risk of disease transmission.

- **Economic Burden**: Communities without reliable access to clean water spend significant time and effort collecting water, diverting resources from other productive activities.

- **Environmental Stress**: Over-extraction and pollution of water sources contribute to environmental degradation, harming ecosystems and biodiversity.

Addressing Water Scarcity:

Efforts to address water scarcity require a comprehensive approach:

- **Infrastructure Development**: Investing in water infrastructure, including wells, boreholes, and water treatment facilities, is essential for expanding access to clean water.

- **Education and Awareness**: Promoting hygiene and sanitation education can empower communities to use water resources more efficiently and safely.

- **Conservation**: Protecting water sources and ecosystems is crucial for ensuring a sustainable supply of clean water.

- **Community Engagement**: Involving communities in water management and decision-making can lead to more equitable and sustainable solutions.

- **Global Cooperation**: Collaborative efforts among nations and international organizations are needed to address transboundary water issues and provide assistance to vulnerable regions.

Understanding the yearly figures and the dire consequences of water scarcity underscores the urgency of ensuring universal access to clean water. By prioritizing investments in water infrastructure, promoting sustainable water management practices, and raising awareness about the importance of clean water, we can work toward a world where clean water is accessible to all, safeguarding health, dignity, and quality of life.

4. Water Scarcity and Its Ramifications

Figure: "Regions Facing Water Scarcity"

Water scarcity is not limited to regions with arid climates. It affects communities worldwide due to over-extraction, pollution, and mismanagement of water resources. Understanding the challenges posed by water scarcity is essential for developing sustainable water management strategies.

- **2020**: In 2020, over 2 billion people lived in countries experiencing high water stress, with more than 4 billion people facing severe water scarcity for at least one month a year.

- **2021**: The impact of climate change, coupled with unsustainable water use practices, exacerbated water scarcity in various regions. Water scarcity led to conflicts and displacement in some areas.

- **2022**: Despite growing awareness of the importance of water conservation, many regions continued to grapple with water scarcity issues, highlighting the need for urgent action.

Water scarcity is not limited to regions with arid climates. It affects communities worldwide due to over-extraction, pollution, and mismanagement of water resources. Understanding the challenges posed by water scarcity is essential for developing sustainable water management strategies.

Challenges Posed by Water Scarcity:

Water scarcity has wide-ranging implications for societies and ecosystems:

- **Agricultural Impacts**: Water scarcity limits crop cultivation and threatens food security, with agriculture consuming the majority of freshwater resources.

- **Conflict Potential**: Competition for limited water resources can lead to tensions and conflicts among communities and even nations.

- **Environmental Stress**: Ecosystems, rivers, and aquatic habitats suffer due to reduced water availability, affecting biodiversity and water-dependent species.

- **Economic Consequences**: Water scarcity can hamper economic growth by limiting industries that rely on water, such as manufacturing and energy production.

Sustainable Water Management Strategies:

Addressing water scarcity requires coordinated efforts and sustainable practices:

- **Water Conservation**: Implementing water-saving technologies and promoting efficient water use in agriculture, industry, and households is essential.

- **Water Recycling and Reuse**: Developing systems for recycling and reusing wastewater can alleviate pressure on freshwater sources.

- **Integrated Water Resource Management**: Adopting integrated approaches to water management, taking into account the needs of all sectors and ecosystems, is vital.

- **Climate Adaptation**: Preparing for the impact of climate change, including prolonged droughts and changing precipitation patterns, is crucial for water resilience.

- **International Cooperation**: Collaborative efforts among nations are necessary to address transboundary water challenges and ensure equitable access.

Understanding the yearly figures and the global nature of water scarcity highlights the urgency of adopting sustainable water management practices. By conserving water, investing in infrastructure, and fostering international cooperation, we can work toward a world where water is a resource accessible to all, ensuring the well-being of both humanity and the environment.

5. Sustainable Agriculture and Food Security

Figure: "Sustainable Farming Practices"

Promoting sustainable agriculture is a key step in addressing hunger and malnutrition. Sustainable farming practices not only increase food production but also protect ecosystems and conserve natural resources. Exploring these practices offers hope for a more food-secure future.

- **2020**: In 2020, approximately 34% of the world's total land area was dedicated to agriculture. However, concerns over soil degradation, loss of biodiversity, and environmental impacts prompted a shift toward sustainable farming practices.

- **2021**: The adoption of sustainable agriculture practices continued to grow, with an increasing number of farmers transitioning to methods that prioritize long-term environmental and food security benefits.

- **2022**: Despite progress, the global agricultural sector faced challenges such as climate change impacts and the need for further adoption of sustainable practices to ensure future food security.

Promoting sustainable agriculture is a key step in addressing hunger and malnutrition. Sustainable farming practices not only increase food production but also protect ecosystems and conserve natural resources. Exploring these practices offers hope for a more food-secure future.

Benefits of Sustainable Agriculture:

Sustainable agriculture offers a range of benefits:

- **Enhanced Soil Health**: Practices like crop rotation and reduced tillage improve soil fertility and reduce erosion.

- **Biodiversity Conservation**: Sustainable farming methods promote biodiversity, preserving essential pollinators and natural pest control agents.

- **Water Conservation**: Efficient irrigation and reduced use of chemical fertilizers and pesticides minimize water pollution and waste.

- **Climate Resilience**: Sustainable practices build resilience to climate change by diversifying crops and enhancing soil carbon storage.

Sustainable Farming Practices:

1. **Crop Rotation**: Rotating crops on the same land reduces soil depletion and pest pressure.

2. **Cover Crops**: Planting cover crops between main crops helps maintain soil fertility and prevent erosion.

3. **Integrated Pest Management**: Using natural predators and pest-resistant crop varieties reduces the need for chemical pesticides.

4. **Agroforestry**: Integrating trees into agricultural landscapes provides shade, reduces soil erosion, and diversifies income sources.

5. **Organic Farming**: Avoiding synthetic chemicals and genetically modified organisms promotes soil health and biodiversity.

Future of Sustainable Agriculture:

The future of sustainable agriculture lies in the continued adoption of these practices and innovations such as precision farming and agtech. Sustainable agriculture not only addresses immediate food security concerns but also ensures the long-term viability of farming for generations to come.

By promoting sustainable farming methods, investing in research and development, and supporting farmers in adopting these practices, we can work toward a future where food security is not only achieved but sustained while protecting the environment and fostering a more resilient agricultural sector.

6. Innovative Solutions

Figure: "Innovations in Clean Water Access"

Innovation plays a crucial role in tackling hunger and thirst. From water purification technologies to novel agricultural techniques, innovative solutions are emerging to address these challenges effectively. These solutions offer inspiration and hope for a brighter and more nourished world.

- **2020**: In 2020, investments in research and innovation led to significant breakthroughs in clean water technologies, such as affordable water purification methods and efficient desalination processes.

- **2021**: The COVID-19 pandemic accelerated the development of touchless water dispensers and contactless payment methods for clean water access, promoting hygiene during the crisis.

- **2022**: Continued innovation in agriculture yielded improved drought-resistant crop varieties and precision farming techniques, helping farmers adapt to changing climate conditions.

Innovation plays a crucial role in tackling hunger and thirst. From water purification technologies to novel agricultural techniques, innovative solutions are emerging to address these challenges effectively. These solutions offer inspiration and hope for a brighter and more nourished world.

Innovations in Clean Water Access:

1. **Solar-Powered Water Purification**: Solar technologies have been harnessed to provide clean drinking water in off-grid and remote areas, making use of abundant sunlight for purification.

2. **Portable Water Filters**: Compact and affordable water filters are becoming more accessible,

allowing individuals to purify water from various sources.

3. **Mobile Apps for Water Quality Monitoring**: Smartphone apps enable communities to monitor and report water quality, ensuring safe drinking water.

4. **Desalination Advancements**: Innovative desalination methods, such as forward osmosis and solar desalination, offer sustainable solutions for freshwater generation in coastal regions.

5. **Atmospheric Water Generators**: Devices that extract water from the air, particularly in arid climates, provide an additional source of clean water.

Innovations in Agriculture:

1. **Drought-Resistant Crops**: Genetic engineering has produced crop varieties that can thrive in water-stressed conditions, increasing resilience to drought.

2. **Precision Agriculture**: Technology-driven farming practices, including the use of sensors and data analytics, optimize resource use and crop yields.

3. **Vertical Farming**: Urban agriculture methods like vertical farming utilize limited space efficiently,

reducing the environmental footprint of food production.

4. **Aquaponics and Hydroponics**: Soil-less farming techniques, such as aquaponics and hydroponics, conserve water while producing fresh produce.

5. **Urban Gardening and Community Farms**: Community-led initiatives promote local food production, fostering self-sufficiency in urban areas.

Future Possibilities:

The future of innovation in addressing hunger and thirst is promising. Emerging technologies such as nanotechnology for water purification and genetic editing for crop improvement hold potential for transformative change. Furthermore, the global community's commitment to sustainability and equitable access to resources will continue to drive progress in these areas.

By supporting research and development, investing in infrastructure, and fostering collaboration among innovators, we can harness the power of innovation to create a world where hunger and thirst are challenges of the past. These solutions not only nourish individuals but also nourish hope for a more prosperous and sustainable future.

Examining hunger and thirst as interconnected challenges highlights the urgent need for coordinated global efforts. By addressing these issues head-on, we can ensure that every person has access to nutritious food and clean water, regardless of where they live. In doing so, we take a significant step toward a more equitable and sustainable world for all.

Hunger-Related Deaths:

- In 2021, an estimated 9.6 million people died of hunger-related causes globally. This includes deaths due to chronic malnutrition, acute food shortages, and related health complications. The COVID-19 pandemic exacerbated food insecurity and hunger in various regions.

Water Scarcity:

- As of 2022, approximately 2.2 billion people, or nearly 30% of the global population, still lacked access to safe drinking water sources, according to the World Health Organization (WHO) and UNICEF. This lack of access increases the risk of waterborne diseases and hampers sanitation efforts.

- Additionally, over 4 billion people faced severe water scarcity for at least one month a year, as per data from the United Nations. This scarcity is due to factors such as over-extraction, pollution, and mismanagement of water resources.

These statistics underscore the urgent need for concerted global efforts to address hunger and water scarcity. It is imperative that we continue to work toward sustainable solutions to ensure that every individual has access to adequate nutrition and clean water for a healthier and more equitable world.

Socioeconomic Factors Contributing to Hunger:

1. **Poverty**: Poverty is one of the most significant drivers of hunger. Individuals and families living in poverty often lack the financial resources to purchase sufficient food. Limited access to education and employment opportunities further exacerbates the cycle of poverty and hunger.

2. **Income Inequality**: Disparities in income distribution can lead to unequal access to food resources. In societies with high income inequality, the wealthy have better access to nutritious food, while the poor struggle to afford basic necessities.

3. **Unemployment and Underemployment**: Lack of job opportunities or underemployment, where individuals work part-time or in low-paying jobs, can result in insufficient income to buy food. This

problem is particularly pronounced in informal economies.

4. **Conflict and Instability**: Regions affected by conflict and political instability often experience disrupted food production and distribution. Displacement of communities and the destruction of infrastructure further worsen food insecurity.

5. **Lack of Infrastructure**: Inadequate infrastructure in rural areas can hinder the transportation and storage of food, leading to wastage and reduced availability. This issue includes poor road networks, limited access to markets, and insufficient cold storage facilities.

Socioeconomic Factors Contributing to Water Scarcity:

1. **Population Growth**: Rapid population growth strains water resources, as more people require access to clean water for drinking, sanitation, and agriculture. Without proper planning and resource management, water scarcity can result.

2. **Urbanization**: The migration of populations from rural to urban areas, driven by economic opportunities, increases water demand in cities. Urbanization often outpaces infrastructure development, leading to water stress in urban centers.

3. **Industrialization**: Industrial and manufacturing activities can consume large quantities of water. In regions with inadequate regulation, industrial water use can deplete local water sources and contribute to scarcity.

4. **Agricultural Practices**: Unsustainable agricultural practices, such as excessive irrigation, chemical use, and monoculture farming, can deplete water resources and harm ecosystems. Sustainable farming practices are crucial to mitigating this issue.

5. **Climate Change**: Changing climate patterns, including prolonged droughts and altered precipitation patterns, can exacerbate water scarcity. Climate-related factors disrupt water availability, affecting both quantity and quality.

6. **Pollution**: Pollution from agricultural runoff, industrial discharges, and untreated sewage can contaminate water sources, making them unusable for consumption. Cleaning up polluted water sources is resource-intensive.

7. **Lack of Access to Infrastructure**: In many regions, inadequate infrastructure for water storage, treatment, and distribution results in water losses and limits access to clean water.

Addressing these socioeconomic factors requires a multifaceted approach, including poverty reduction, improved access to education and healthcare, sustainable economic development, conflict resolution, and sustainable resource management. By addressing these root causes, we can work toward a future where hunger and water scarcity are significantly reduced, if not eliminated, on a global scale.

Section 4: Access to Healthcare

Access to healthcare is a fundamental human right, yet disparities in healthcare access persist across different regions and demographics. This section delves into the complex landscape of healthcare access, exploring the factors that contribute to these disparities and their far-reaching consequences.

1. Regional Disparities

- **2020**: In 2020, significant regional disparities in healthcare access were evident. While some countries boasted robust healthcare systems with universal coverage, others struggled to provide even basic medical services to their populations.

- **2021**: The COVID-19 pandemic further highlighted regional disparities in healthcare, with some nations able to rapidly deploy vaccines and medical resources, while others faced critical shortages and limited access to healthcare infrastructure.

- **2022**: Efforts to address regional healthcare disparities continued, with international organizations and governments working to improve healthcare infrastructure and access in underserved areas.

2. Demographic Disparities in Healthcare Access

Figure: "Demographic Disparities in Healthcare Access"

- **2020**: In 2020, demographic disparities in healthcare access persisted, revealing the stark inequalities in healthcare delivery. Vulnerable populations, including low-income communities, ethnic minorities, refugees, and other marginalized groups, continued to face significant barriers to accessing quality healthcare services.

- **2021**: The COVID-19 pandemic laid bare the harsh realities of demographic disparities in healthcare. Minority and economically disadvantaged communities were disproportionately affected by the pandemic, with higher infection rates, more severe outcomes, and reduced access to critical medical resources.

- **2022**: In response to the pandemic's glaring disparities, initiatives aimed at addressing demographic disparities in healthcare gained momentum. Governments, NGOs, and healthcare institutions implemented strategies to expand outreach programs, promote cultural competency in healthcare settings, and increase funding for community clinics that serve underserved populations.

Key Factors Contributing to Demographic Disparities in Healthcare Access:

1. **Economic Inequality**: Low-income individuals and families often struggle to afford healthcare services. The cost of medical care, medications, and health insurance premiums can place significant financial burdens on economically disadvantaged communities.

2. **Health Literacy**: Lower levels of education can result in limited health literacy. Understanding health information, navigating healthcare systems, and making informed healthcare decisions become challenging for individuals with limited education.

3. **Employment Status**: Access to healthcare is often tied to employment. Those in non-traditional or precarious employment arrangements, including gig workers and those without stable jobs, may lack access to employer-sponsored healthcare benefits.

4. **Racial and Ethnic Disparities**: Minority populations, particularly racial and ethnic minorities, often face disparities in healthcare access. Discrimination, bias, and unequal

treatment within healthcare systems contribute to these disparities.

5. **Geographic Location**: The geographic location of individuals can significantly impact healthcare access. Rural and remote areas often lack healthcare facilities, and long travel distances can delay or deter individuals from seeking necessary medical care.

6. **Language and Cultural Barriers**: Cultural and language barriers can create obstacles to healthcare access. Providing culturally competent care and offering interpreter services are essential steps in addressing these disparities.

7. **Immigration Status**: Undocumented immigrants and refugees often face challenges in accessing healthcare due to their immigration status. Fear of deportation and lack of insurance coverage can deter them from seeking medical care.

Addressing these regional and demographic disparities in healthcare access requires comprehensive efforts to promote equitable healthcare for all individuals, regardless of their background or circumstances. Efforts to bridge these disparities contribute to a more just and inclusive healthcare system.

Consequences of Limited Access to Healthcare and Medical Treatment

Limited access to healthcare and medical treatment can have profound and far-reaching consequences, affecting individuals, communities, and entire societies. Here, we provide comprehensive examples of these consequences, shedding light on the gravity of the issue:

1. **Higher Mortality Rates**: One of the most immediate and tragic consequences of limited access to healthcare is higher mortality rates. Individuals who cannot access timely medical care for acute illnesses or chronic conditions are at a significantly greater risk of dying prematurely. This includes conditions like heart disease, diabetes, and certain types of cancer, where early detection and intervention are critical.

2. **Increased Disease Burden**: Limited access to healthcare can lead to a higher burden of preventable diseases within a population. For example, lack of access to vaccines and routine immunizations can result in outbreaks of infectious diseases such as measles or polio. This not only affects the health of individuals but also places strain on healthcare systems and resources.

3. **Worsening Health Inequalities**: Healthcare disparities exacerbate existing health inequalities

within society. Vulnerable populations, including low-income individuals, racial and ethnic minorities, and those with disabilities, are disproportionately affected. These disparities can lead to a cycle of poverty, reduced educational attainment, and diminished economic opportunities.

4. **Delayed Diagnosis and Treatment**: Limited access to healthcare often translates into delayed diagnosis and treatment. For conditions like cancer, early detection can be a matter of life and death. Delayed diagnosis may result in more advanced stages of disease, reducing the chances of successful treatment and survival.

5. **Increased Healthcare Costs**: Paradoxically, limited access to healthcare can lead to higher overall healthcare costs. When individuals cannot access preventive care or early intervention, they may eventually seek treatment in emergency departments, where care is more expensive. This places a burden on the healthcare system and can lead to increased costs for both individuals and governments.

6. **Economic Impact**: The economic consequences of limited healthcare access are substantial. Illness and disability due to untreated or poorly managed conditions can lead to reduced productivity and missed workdays. Families may face financial

hardships due to medical bills, further entrenching them in poverty.

7. **Mental Health Implications**: Limited access to mental healthcare can have severe mental health implications. Individuals facing mental health challenges may not receive the necessary support, leading to worsening conditions, including depression, anxiety, and even suicide.

8. **Maternal and Child Health**: Limited access to prenatal care and obstetric services can lead to adverse outcomes in maternal and child health. Higher rates of maternal mortality, preterm births, and low birth weights are observed in areas with inadequate access to maternal healthcare.

9. **Public Health Threats**: Limited healthcare access can contribute to public health threats. For instance, individuals without access to HIV testing and treatment may unknowingly transmit the virus to others. Similarly, lack of access to treatment for tuberculosis can result in drug-resistant strains of the disease, posing a greater public health risk.

10. **Social Unrest**: In extreme cases, limited access to healthcare can lead to social unrest and political instability. Communities that perceive unequal access to healthcare as an injustice may protest or engage in civil unrest, demanding better healthcare infrastructure and services.

These examples illustrate the multifaceted and cascading effects of limited access to healthcare and medical treatment. Addressing these disparities requires comprehensive efforts, including policy changes, increased healthcare infrastructure, improved education, and a commitment to ensuring that healthcare is a universal right, not a privilege.

Discuss the role of healthcare in improving overall well-being.

Healthcare plays a pivotal role in enhancing and sustaining overall well-being. It encompasses a broad spectrum of services and interventions aimed at promoting physical, mental, and social health. Here, we delve into the multifaceted role of healthcare in improving well-being:

1. **Preventive Care**: Healthcare offers preventive measures such as vaccinations, screenings, and regular check-ups. By identifying health risks early, individuals can make informed lifestyle choices and receive timely interventions to prevent the onset of diseases.

2. **Early Detection and Treatment**: Regular healthcare visits facilitate the early detection of illnesses. Early diagnosis often leads to more effective and less invasive treatments, increasing

the chances of recovery and reducing the impact of diseases on overall well-being.

3. **Management of Chronic Conditions**: For individuals living with chronic conditions like diabetes, hypertension, or asthma, healthcare provides essential support in managing these conditions. Proper management helps maintain a good quality of life and prevents complications.

4. **Mental Health Support**: Healthcare services encompass mental health support, including therapy and counseling. Addressing mental health concerns is crucial for overall well-being, as it enhances emotional resilience and coping mechanisms.

5. **Access to Medications**: Healthcare ensures access to medications and treatments, which are essential for managing various health conditions. Proper medication management can significantly improve the well-being of individuals with chronic diseases.

6. **Health Education**: Healthcare professionals offer health education, empowering individuals to make informed decisions about their well-being. This includes guidance on nutrition, exercise, stress management, and healthy lifestyle choices.

7. **Pregnancy and Maternal Care**: Healthcare plays a vital role in ensuring the health of expectant mothers and their infants. Prenatal care, safe

deliveries, and postnatal support contribute to the well-being of both mother and child.

8. **Emergency Care**: Healthcare provides critical emergency services that can be life-saving. Rapid response to accidents, injuries, and acute medical conditions is essential for preserving well-being.

9. **Promoting Social Well-Being**: Healthcare interventions extend beyond physical health. Social workers and counselors assist individuals and families in navigating social challenges, such as domestic violence, substance abuse, and homelessness, which can significantly impact overall well-being.

10. **Supporting Aging Populations**: Healthcare services cater to the needs of aging populations. Geriatric care focuses on maintaining independence, managing age-related conditions, and ensuring a high quality of life for older adults.

11. **Community Health Initiatives**: Healthcare institutions often engage in community health initiatives, addressing broader determinants of well-being. These efforts include health education in schools, promoting healthy environments, and addressing social inequalities.

12. **Disease Outbreak Control**: During disease outbreaks, healthcare systems play a critical role in preventing the spread of infections and

providing care to affected individuals. This safeguards the well-being of entire communities.

13. **Health Equity**: Healthcare strives to promote health equity, ensuring that all individuals, regardless of their background or circumstances, have access to essential healthcare services. Addressing disparities contributes to greater well-being for society as a whole.

In essence, healthcare serves as a cornerstone for enhancing overall well-being by addressing health needs, preventing illness, and providing support and care when needed. It empowers individuals to lead healthier, more fulfilling lives and contributes to the collective well-being of communities and nations.

Section 5: Wars and Conflicts

1: Ancient Battles and Empires

Ancient history bears witness to the rise and fall of powerful empires, often forged on the battlefield. The conquests of Alexander the Great stand as a testament to the audacity of ancient warriors. His campaigns stretched from Greece to Egypt, Persia to India, leaving a legacy of Hellenistic culture in their wake. Likewise, the Roman Empire's inexorable expansion across Europe, Asia, and Africa was driven by military might. The Punic Wars against Carthage, led by generals like Hannibal, showcased strategic brilliance and the immense human cost of war. These ancient conflicts reveal the enduring fascination with territorial conquest and the seeds of modern geopolitics.

2: Medieval Warfare and Feudalism

The medieval era was marked by feudal systems, chivalric codes, and incessant conflict. The Crusades, driven by religious fervor and imperial ambition, saw European knights venture to the Holy Land in a series of brutal clashes. The Hundred Years' War, fought over dynastic claims, exemplified the shift from medieval chivalry to evolving military tactics, including the use of longbows. Feudalism, the dominant socio-economic structure, influenced the organization of armies and the dynamics of medieval warfare, leaving an indelible mark on the Middle Ages.

3: Early Modern Wars and Colonialism

The early modern period witnessed a transformation in warfare as the world experienced the age of exploration, colonization, and the emergence of nation-states. The Thirty Years' War, a complex web of religious and political conflicts, devastated Europe and reshaped the balance of power. The American Revolution, driven by ideals of independence and democracy, challenged colonial rule and inspired movements worldwide. The Opium Wars highlighted the clash of interests between China and Western powers. These conflicts set the stage for modern imperialism, nationalism, and the pursuit of global dominance.

4: World Wars and Global Conflicts

The 20th century bore witness to two cataclysmic world wars, profoundly altering the course of history. World War I, sparked by political entanglements and alliances, introduced industrialized warfare, including trench warfare and chemical weapons. World War II, with its devastating scale and genocide, underscored the consequences of unchecked aggression. The aftermath led to the Cold War, a tense ideological standoff, and numerous regional conflicts. These global conflicts redefined geopolitics, international institutions, and the pursuit of peace in a nuclear age.

5: Contemporary Conflicts and Geopolitics

Contemporary conflicts continue to shape the geopolitical landscape. The Middle East, a crucible of tensions, has seen conflicts like the Gulf War, Iraq War, and the ongoing Israeli-Palestinian conflict. The Balkans grappled with ethnic conflicts and the dissolution of Yugoslavia. Africa witnessed struggles for independence, civil wars, and humanitarian crises. Asia, from the Korean Peninsula to the South China Sea, remains a hotspot of regional tensions. The role of superpowers, alliances, and international organizations in mediating or exacerbating these conflicts is a central theme.

6: Lessons Learned and Paths to Peace

Amidst the tumult of wars and conflicts, valuable lessons have emerged. Diplomacy, exemplified by treaties like the Treaty of Versailles and the United Nations Charter, seeks to prevent future conflicts. International organizations such as the United Nations strive to mediate disputes and promote peacekeeping efforts. The pursuit of nuclear disarmament and arms control reflects a collective commitment to preventing catastrophic conflicts. As we navigate the complex tapestry of human conflicts, these lessons underscore the imperative of dialogue, diplomacy, and cooperation on a global scale to secure a more peaceful future.

In exploring the history of wars and conflicts, this section aims to provide a comprehensive understanding of how these pivotal events have shaped human societies, cultures, and the ongoing quest for peace in an ever-changing world.

Environmental and Societal Consequences

Armed conflicts have far-reaching repercussions that extend beyond the battlefield, leaving an enduring imprint on both the environment and society. In this subsection, we delve into the intricate web of consequences arising from wars and conflicts.

Environmental Consequences

1. **Devastated Landscapes**: Wars transform landscapes into battlefields, with scarred earth, destroyed infrastructure, and contaminated soil. The aftermath often necessitates extensive environmental rehabilitation efforts.

2. **Pollution and Contamination**: The use of explosives, chemicals, and munitions releases pollutants into the environment, contaminating water sources and soil. The long-term effects on ecosystems and public health are significant.

3. **Displacement and Deforestation**: Armed conflicts frequently result in mass displacement, leading to deforestation as refugees seek shelter and resources. This has cascading effects on biodiversity and carbon emissions.

4. **Resource Exploitation**: Conflict zones become hotbeds for illegal resource extraction, including timber and minerals, funding further violence and perpetuating environmental degradation.

Societal Consequences

1. **Humanitarian Crises**: Armed conflicts give rise to humanitarian crises, displacing millions, causing food shortages, and straining healthcare systems. Innocent civilians, especially women and children, bear the brunt of these crises.

2. **Psychological Trauma**: The psychological toll of war extends to combatants and civilians alike, leading to conditions like post-traumatic stress disorder (PTSD) and affecting generations.

3. **Disrupted Education**: Conflict disrupts education systems, robbing generations of opportunities and perpetuating cycles of poverty and instability.

4. **Cultural Heritage Loss**: Centuries of cultural heritage can be destroyed in moments of conflict, erasing vital aspects of identity and history.

5. **Economic Fallout**: Economies in conflict zones suffer severe setbacks, affecting employment, infrastructure, and the overall well-being of communities.

6. **Social Cohesion Erosion**: Communities torn apart by conflict often struggle to rebuild social cohesion, exacerbating divisions and impeding recovery.

7. **Refugee Crisis**: Armed conflicts generate massive refugee crises, straining neighboring countries and leading to global displacement challenges.

Paths to Recovery and Reconciliation

Despite the profound consequences of armed conflicts, societies have shown resilience in rebuilding and reconciling. International humanitarian organizations provide aid, support, and mediation efforts. Post-conflict reconciliation, truth and reconciliation commissions, and transitional justice mechanisms aim to heal societies and prevent future conflicts. Additionally, addressing environmental damage and promoting sustainable development are integral to the recovery process.

This subsection underscores the intricate relationship between armed conflicts, their environmental and societal consequences, and the imperative of forging paths to recovery, healing, and reconciliation in conflict-ridden regions around the world.

Promoting Peace and Preventing Future Conflicts

Amidst the harrowing history of wars and conflicts, humanity has continually sought pathways to peace and strategies to avert future hostilities. This subsection explores the multifaceted efforts aimed at promoting peace and preventing the recurrence of conflicts.

Diplomacy and Conflict Resolution

1. **Negotiation and Diplomacy**: Diplomatic negotiations and peace talks, often facilitated by international organizations and mediators, serve as vital tools for resolving disputes peacefully.

2. **Conflict Mediation**: Mediation efforts bring conflicting parties to the table, fostering dialogue, and reconciliation. These initiatives aim to address grievances, build trust, and seek mutually acceptable solutions.

3. **Peace Treaties**: Historic peace treaties, such as the Treaty of Westphalia and the Camp David Accords, have played pivotal roles in ending protracted conflicts and establishing frameworks for lasting peace.

International Organizations

1. **United Nations**: The United Nations (UN) and its various agencies work tirelessly to prevent conflicts, provide humanitarian assistance, and promote diplomacy on a global scale.

2. **Peacekeeping Missions**: UN peacekeeping missions deploy troops and observers to conflict

zones, acting as stabilizing forces and facilitating peace processes.

3. **Conflict Prevention**: The UN engages in conflict prevention efforts, addressing root causes such as poverty, inequality, and political instability to mitigate the risk of conflict.

Arms Control and Disarmament

1. **Nuclear Disarmament**: Efforts to reduce nuclear arsenals through treaties like the Treaty on the Non-Proliferation of Nuclear Weapons (NPT) aim to prevent catastrophic conflicts.

2. **Conventional Arms Control**: Agreements and treaties seek to limit the proliferation of conventional weapons, reducing the potential for armed conflict.

Humanitarian Aid and Development

1. **Humanitarian Assistance**: Organizations like the Red Cross provide critical aid to conflict-affected populations, delivering food, medical care, and shelter.

2. **Reconstruction and Development**: Post-conflict reconstruction and development initiatives aim to rebuild infrastructure, restore economies, and create stable societies.

Education and Advocacy

1. **Peace Education**: Promoting peace education in schools and communities instills conflict resolution skills, tolerance, and the importance of non-violence.

2. **Advocacy and Awareness**: Civil society organizations and activists advocate for peace, raising awareness about the human cost of conflicts and the need for global cooperation.

Technology and Early Warning Systems

1. **Early Warning Systems**: Technological advancements enable early warning systems that can detect potential conflicts, allowing for timely interventions.

2. **Digital Diplomacy**: Digital platforms and social media facilitate diplomacy and peacebuilding efforts, fostering dialogue among diverse stakeholders.

Transitional Justice and Reconciliation

1. **Truth and Reconciliation Commissions**: Post-conflict societies often establish truth and reconciliation commissions to address past atrocities, promote healing, and prevent future grievances.

2. **Justice Mechanisms**: Holding perpetrators of war crimes accountable through international tribunals contributes to establishing a culture of accountability.

Civil Society Engagement

1. **People-to-People Initiatives**: Grassroots efforts, involving citizens from conflicting parties in dialogue and cooperation, promote peace from the ground up.

2. **Track II Diplomacy**: Non-official diplomatic channels facilitate discreet discussions and build trust between conflicting parties.

By examining these diverse efforts, this subsection emphasizes the collective commitment to peacebuilding and conflict prevention, demonstrating that while wars have left scars on history, humanity's resolve to foster peace and prevent future conflicts remains unwavering.

Section 6: Civilian Casualties

Non-Military Weapons

The impact of conflicts extends far beyond the battlefield, affecting civilian populations in numerous ways. This subsection explores the consequences of non-military weapons, which include economic sanctions, cyberattacks, and other forms of coercion.

Economic Sanctions

Economic sanctions, often employed as diplomatic tools, can have unintended and severe consequences for civilian populations caught in the crossfire of international disputes.

1. **Humanitarian Impact**: Economic sanctions can lead to severe shortages of essential goods, including food, medical supplies, and clean water. Civilians, especially the vulnerable and marginalized, bear the brunt of these shortages, resulting in malnutrition, disease, and even death.

2. **Social Disruption**: Economic hardships resulting from sanctions can disrupt social systems and erode the fabric of communities. As unemployment rises and poverty deepens, families struggle to maintain basic living standards, leading to social unrest and increased vulnerability, particularly among children and the elderly.

3. **Economic Stagnation**: Sanctions can hinder economic development and recovery, prolonging the suffering of civilians. In conflict-affected regions, these restrictions can stall post-conflict reconstruction efforts, trapping communities in a cycle of poverty and instability.

Cyberattacks

In the digital age, cyberattacks have emerged as potent non-military weapons, with consequences that extend well beyond the virtual realm.

1. **Critical Infrastructure**: Cyberattacks targeting critical infrastructure, such as power grids, healthcare systems, and transportation networks, can disrupt essential services. In hospitals, for instance, a cyberattack may compromise patient care, putting lives at risk.

2. **Data Breaches**: Attacks on data and personal information can jeopardize individual privacy and security. Stolen data may be used for identity theft, financial fraud, or other malicious purposes, impacting the affected individuals for years to come.

3. **Economic Fallout**: Cyberattacks on businesses can lead to financial losses, layoffs, and even bankruptcies. When civilians lose their livelihoods due to such attacks, the consequences reverberate throughout their lives and communities.

Subsection 2: Hate, Discrimination, and Injustice

In times of conflict and beyond, the perpetuation of hate, discrimination, and injustice can have profound and enduring effects on civilian populations.

Hate Crimes

Hate crimes, driven by prejudice and animosity, not only inflict physical harm but also scar the social fabric of societies.

1. **Targeted Violence**: Hate crimes involve targeted violence against individuals or groups based on their ethnicity, religion, race, gender, or other characteristics. These acts can cause physical injuries, psychological trauma, and, in some cases, death.

2. **Social Division**: Hate crimes create divisions within communities, eroding trust and cohesion. Fear and mistrust among different groups can persist long after the conflict has ended, hindering reconciliation efforts.

3. **Psychological Impact**: Victims and witnesses of hate crimes often experience profound psychological distress. The trauma can lead to anxiety, depression, and post-traumatic stress disorder, affecting mental health and well-being.

Discrimination

Discrimination, whether systemic or individual, perpetuates inequality and marginalization, with far-reaching consequences.

1. **Systemic Discrimination**: Discriminatory laws, policies, and practices can marginalize specific

groups, denying them access to essential services, opportunities, and justice. The enduring effects of systemic discrimination can persist for generations.

2. **Economic Impact**: Discrimination in employment, education, and housing can limit economic opportunities for affected individuals and communities. This economic disenfranchisement perpetuates cycles of poverty, making it difficult for marginalized groups to escape their circumstances.

3. **Social Exclusion**: Discrimination isolates individuals and groups, leading to social exclusion and alienation. When communities are divided along lines of ethnicity, religion, or other factors, trust erodes, and social cohesion is compromised.

Injustice and Impunity

Injustice occurs when perpetrators of crimes against civilians go unpunished, undermining trust in the legal system and society as a whole.

1. **Impunity for Crimes**: When individuals or groups responsible for crimes against civilians are not held accountable, it erodes confidence in the justice system. Victims and survivors may feel that their suffering goes unrecognized and unaddressed.

2. **Psychological Trauma**: The trauma of experiencing or witnessing injustice can have long-lasting psychological effects. It can lead to feelings of helplessness, anger, and despair, impacting mental health and well-being.

3. **Social and Community Disruption**: Injustice can disrupt social structures and community bonds. The lack of accountability for crimes can lead to grievances and conflicts that persist for generations, hindering reconciliation efforts.

This comprehensive exploration of the consequences of non-military weapons and the enduring harm caused by hate, discrimination, and injustice underscores the need for concerted efforts to protect civilian populations during and after conflicts, and to promote inclusive and just societies.

Highlighting Case Studies and Historical Events

To provide a deeper understanding of the toll on civilians resulting from non-military weapons, hate, discrimination, and injustice, this section presents case studies and historical events that exemplify the profound impact on civilian populations.

Case Study 1: The Effects of Economic Sanctions

In the 1990s, Iraq endured extensive economic sanctions following the Gulf War. These sanctions, while intended to pressure the government, had severe consequences for civilians:

- **Humanitarian Crisis**: The sanctions led to a humanitarian crisis, with millions of Iraqis facing food and medicine shortages. Malnutrition and disease, especially among children, surged.

- **Social Unrest**: Economic hardship led to social unrest and instability. Unemployment rates soared, and many Iraqis struggled to meet basic needs, including clean water and healthcare.

- **Long-Term Consequences**: Even after the sanctions were lifted, Iraq faced long-term challenges in rebuilding its economy and healthcare system. The toll on civilian populations, particularly children, left a lasting impact.

Case Study 2: Cyberattacks on Critical Infrastructure

In 2015, Ukraine experienced a cyberattack on its power grid. This incident highlighted the real-world consequences of cyber warfare:

- **Power Outages**: The cyberattack caused widespread power outages in Ukraine during the winter. Civilians, including vulnerable populations, faced freezing temperatures without heating or electricity.

- **Disrupted Services**: Healthcare facilities, transportation networks, and essential services were disrupted, affecting civilians' access to medical care and daily necessities.

- **Fear and Uncertainty**: The cyberattack created fear and uncertainty among the civilian population. Trust in critical infrastructure systems was shaken, and the psychological impact persisted even after power was restored.

Historical Event: The Rwandan Genocide

The Rwandan Genocide in 1994 was fueled by hate and discrimination, resulting in the mass killing of civilians:

- **Hate Crimes**: The genocide involved hate crimes targeted at the Tutsi ethnic group. Thousands of civilians were brutally murdered based on their ethnicity.

- **Social Division**: The genocide left deep social divisions in Rwanda. Reconciliation efforts have been ongoing to heal the wounds and bridge the divides.

- **Psychological Trauma**: Survivors of the genocide experienced severe psychological trauma. Many suffer from post-traumatic stress disorder and other mental health issues.

Historical Event: Apartheid in South Africa

Apartheid in South Africa, which persisted for decades, was a system of legalized discrimination:

- **Systemic Discrimination**: Apartheid laws enforced systemic discrimination against non-white South Africans, denying them equal rights and access to resources.

- **Economic Inequality**: Apartheid led to economic inequality, with non-white populations facing limited economic opportunities and access to education and healthcare.

- **Social Exclusion**: Apartheid created social exclusion, dividing communities along racial lines and undermining social cohesion.

These case studies and historical events serve as poignant reminders of the far-reaching and enduring consequences of non-military weapons, hate, discrimination, and injustice on civilian populations. They underscore the imperative of promoting peace, justice, and equality to protect and uplift all members of society.

Discussing the Importance of Promoting Tolerance and Equality

Promoting tolerance and equality is not just a moral imperative; it is an essential foundation for building peaceful, inclusive, and prosperous societies. In a world where conflicts, discrimination, and injustices persist, understanding the significance of these values is paramount.

1. **Social Harmony and Cohesion**

Tolerance and equality foster social harmony and cohesion. When individuals from diverse backgrounds, with varying beliefs, and of different identities coexist harmoniously, communities become stronger. Social cohesion reduces the likelihood of conflicts and promotes a sense of belonging among all members of society.

2. **Conflict Prevention**

Discrimination and inequality are often root causes of conflicts. Promoting tolerance and equality can prevent the escalation of tensions and violence. Inclusive societies are less susceptible to internal strife and are better equipped to resolve disputes peacefully.

3. **Economic Prosperity**

Equality is closely tied to economic prosperity. When individuals have equal access to education, employment opportunities, and resources, economies thrive. Inclusive economic policies that promote equality can lead to increased productivity and innovation.

4. Human Dignity

Every individual has inherent worth and dignity. Promoting tolerance and equality upholds these principles by ensuring that all people, regardless of their background, are treated with respect and fairness. This contributes to the preservation of human dignity.

5. Social Justice

Tolerance and equality are cornerstones of social justice. They address historical and systemic injustices, working to level the playing field for marginalized and discriminated groups. Social justice leads to a more equitable distribution of resources and opportunities.

6. Health and Well-being

Discrimination and inequality can have detrimental effects on physical and mental health. Promoting tolerance and equality supports the well-being of all individuals. It reduces the stress and trauma associated with discrimination and fosters a sense of security.

7. Education and Empowerment

Education is a powerful tool for promoting tolerance and equality. Inclusive education systems empower individuals to challenge stereotypes, embrace diversity, and become advocates for justice. An educated and informed populace is more likely to reject discrimination.

8. Global Peace

On a global scale, promoting tolerance and equality is essential for peace. International conflicts often arise from inequality and injustice. By addressing these root causes and fostering cooperation, the international community can work towards a more peaceful world.

9. Cultural Enrichment

Tolerance allows for the celebration of diverse cultures, languages, and traditions. This cultural enrichment enriches societies and broadens perspectives. It encourages the exchange of ideas and fosters creativity.

10. Future Generations

Promoting tolerance and equality is an investment in the future. By instilling these values in younger generations, we create a legacy of inclusion and justice. These generations are more likely to continue the work of building equitable societies.

In conclusion, the importance of promoting tolerance and equality cannot be overstated. These values are the pillars upon which just, inclusive, and peaceful societies are built. Embracing tolerance and equality not only benefits individuals but also strengthens communities, nations, and the world as a whole. It is a collective responsibility to champion these values and work towards a better, fairer future for all.

Section 7: Criminal Activities

Criminal activities have wide-ranging and profound impacts on society and the environment. Investigating the influence of criminal groups, gangs, and mafia is essential to understanding the challenges they pose and devising effective strategies to mitigate their detrimental effects.

1. Criminal Networks and Their Reach

Criminal groups operate both locally and globally, transcending borders and jurisdictions. They engage in various illicit activities, including drug trafficking, human smuggling, arms trade, and more. Understanding the extent of their reach is crucial for law enforcement agencies and policymakers.

2. Socioeconomic Impacts

Criminal activities have significant socioeconomic impacts:

- **Economic Drain**: Illicit economies divert resources away from legitimate businesses and investments. This drains the economy and hinders growth.

- **Poverty and Vulnerability**: Criminal groups often exploit vulnerable populations, trapping individuals in cycles of poverty and crime. This perpetuates social inequalities.

- **Undermining Institutions**: Corruption and infiltration of legal institutions by criminal networks erode trust in government and the rule of law.

3. Violence and Insecurity

Criminal groups, gangs, and mafia are often associated with violence and insecurity:

- **Homicide Rates**: Areas with high criminal activities tend to have elevated homicide rates, leading to loss of life and public fear.

- **Displacement**: Violence and insecurity can displace communities, causing them to flee their homes, disrupting their lives, and straining resources in host regions.

- **Impact on Youth**: Criminal groups recruit young individuals, luring them into a life of crime and violence, further perpetuating cycles of instability.

4. Environmental Exploitation

Criminal activities also have environmental consequences:

- **Illegal Resource Extraction**: Criminal organizations engage in illegal logging, mining, and wildlife trafficking, contributing to deforestation, habitat loss, and endangering species.

- **Pollution and Waste**: Illicit industries often disregard environmental regulations, resulting in pollution, chemical spills, and improper disposal of hazardous waste.

- **Poaching and Wildlife Trade**: Criminal networks drive the illegal trade in endangered species, leading to the depletion of biodiversity and disruption of ecosystems.

5. Trafficking and Exploitation

Criminal groups profit from human trafficking and exploitation:

- **Human Trafficking**: Victims of human trafficking, often coerced or deceived, suffer physical and psychological trauma, while criminals profit from their misery.

- **Exploitative Labor**: Criminal organizations exploit vulnerable individuals through forced labor, perpetuating cycles of poverty and suffering.

6. The Nexus with Corruption

Corruption often enables criminal activities to thrive:

- **Compromised Authorities**: Corrupt officials provide protection and support to criminal networks, making it challenging to dismantle them.

- **Undermining Governance**: Corruption undermines governance, erodes public trust, and hampers the ability of governments to address criminal activities effectively.

7. Efforts to Combat Criminal Networks

Understanding the influence of criminal groups and mafia is vital for developing strategies to combat them:

- **Law Enforcement**: Collaborative efforts among law enforcement agencies, both nationally and internationally, are crucial for dismantling criminal networks.

- **Community Engagement**: Engaging communities affected by criminal activities is essential for prevention and reporting.

- **Anti-Corruption Measures**: Strengthening anti-corruption measures and promoting transparency in institutions can reduce the influence of criminal groups.

Investigating the multifaceted influence of criminal groups, gangs, and mafia is essential for protecting society and the environment. Efforts to combat these activities require a coordinated, multidimensional approach that addresses both their immediate and underlying causes.

Examples of Criminal Activities That Harm Communities and Ecosystems

Criminal activities have far-reaching consequences, often causing harm to both communities and ecosystems. Here are some specific examples that illustrate the detrimental impact of criminal actions:

1. Drug Trafficking and Violence

- **Example**: Drug cartels in Central and South America engage in drug trafficking, leading to violence, displacement, and instability. These criminal groups often seize land for illegal cultivation, causing deforestation and habitat destruction. Additionally, the chemicals used in drug production harm local ecosystems and contaminate water sources.

2. Illegal Logging and Deforestation

- **Example**: Illegal logging operations in the Amazon rainforest result in deforestation, disrupting ecosystems and causing the loss of biodiversity. These activities often involve corruption, as criminal groups bribe officials to obtain logging permits. The long-term effects include soil erosion, disrupted water cycles, and reduced carbon sequestration.

3. Wildlife Trafficking

- **Example**: Poaching and wildlife trafficking networks, operating globally, target endangered species for their body parts, skins, and exotic pets. This leads to the depletion of wildlife populations, disrupts ecosystems, and threatens species with extinction. Additionally, trafficking routes can facilitate the spread of diseases from wildlife to humans.

4. Illegal Fishing and Overfishing

- **Example**: Criminal organizations engage in illegal fishing and overfishing, depleting marine resources and threatening the livelihoods of coastal communities. The use of destructive fishing methods, such as dynamite or cyanide, damages coral reefs and marine habitats, impacting marine biodiversity.

5. Human Trafficking and Exploitation

- **Example**: Human trafficking networks exploit vulnerable individuals, subjecting them to forced labor, sexual exploitation, and other forms of abuse. This harms communities by trapping people in cycles of poverty and suffering. The criminal organizations profit from the exploitation of human lives.

6. Cybercrime and Environmental Damage

- **Example**: Cybercriminals target critical infrastructure, including energy grids and industrial facilities. Disruptions to these systems can lead to environmental damage, such as chemical leaks or oil spills. These incidents harm ecosystems and can have long-lasting ecological consequences.

7. Organized Poaching and Ivory Trade

- **Example**: Organized criminal networks engage in poaching elephants and rhinos for their ivory. The ivory trade fuels corruption, funds armed conflicts, and threatens the existence of these iconic species. The loss of large herbivores can disrupt ecosystems and affect plant communities.

8. Artifacts and Cultural Heritage Theft

- **Example**: Criminals steal cultural artifacts and heritage items, including ancient sculptures and archaeological treasures. This erases cultural history, robs communities of their heritage, and can lead to the destruction of archaeological sites and cultural landmarks.

9. Corruption and Environmental Exploitation

- **Example**: Corruption within government agencies allows criminal groups to exploit natural resources illegally, such as mining or logging in protected areas. This not only harms ecosystems but also diverts revenue that could benefit communities through legitimate resource management.

These examples underscore the multifaceted impact of criminal activities on communities and ecosystems. Criminal networks often exploit both human and natural resources, causing long-term harm that extends far beyond the immediate consequences of their actions. Addressing these issues requires a concerted effort involving law enforcement, conservation efforts, community engagement, and international cooperation.

Discussing Strategies for Combating Organized Crime and Ensuring Safety

Combatting organized crime is a complex and multifaceted challenge that requires a comprehensive approach involving law enforcement, government agencies, communities, and international cooperation.

Here, we discuss strategies aimed at dismantling criminal networks and ensuring the safety of communities and society at large:

1. Strengthening Law Enforcement

- **Multi-Agency Cooperation**: Encourage collaboration among different law enforcement agencies at the local, national, and international levels to share intelligence, resources, and expertise.

- **Training and Resources**: Provide ongoing training and necessary resources to law enforcement personnel to equip them with the skills needed to combat organized crime effectively.

2. Targeting Financial Networks

- **Financial Investigations**: Investigate the financial aspects of criminal operations, including money laundering and asset seizures, to disrupt the financial backbone of criminal organizations.

- **International Banking Regulations**: Implement international banking regulations to track and freeze assets linked to criminal networks, limiting their ability to launder money.

3. Community Engagement

- **Community Policing**: Promote community policing initiatives that build trust between law enforcement and local communities. Encourage residents to report suspicious activities.

- **Support for Vulnerable Communities**: Invest in programs that address the root causes of crime, such as poverty, lack of education, and unemployment, to reduce vulnerability to criminal exploitation.

4. Legislative Reforms

- **Tougher Penalties**: Enact and enforce stricter penalties for individuals involved in organized crime, including leaders, financiers, and lower-level members.

- **Asset Forfeiture Laws**: Strengthen laws that allow for the seizure of assets obtained through criminal activities, ensuring that criminals do not benefit from their illicit gains.

5. International Cooperation

- **Interpol and Europol**: Collaborate with international law enforcement agencies like Interpol and Europol to share intelligence and coordinate efforts to combat transnational organized crime.

- **Mutual Legal Assistance Treaties (MLATs)**: Sign MLATs with other countries to facilitate the extradition of criminals and the sharing of evidence across borders.

6. Disrupting Supply Chains

- **Targeting Key Trafficking Routes**: Focus efforts on disrupting the key supply routes and networks used by criminal organizations involved in drug trafficking, human smuggling, and other illicit activities.

- **Innovative Surveillance Technologies**: Employ advanced surveillance technologies, including satellite imagery and drones, to monitor and disrupt criminal operations in remote or inaccessible areas.

7. Empowering Informants

- **Witness Protection Programs**: Establish witness protection programs to encourage individuals with knowledge of criminal activities to come forward without fear of retaliation.

- **Whistleblower Incentives**: Create incentives for insiders to expose criminal organizations by offering financial rewards and legal protections.

8. Public Awareness

- **Education Campaigns**: Raise public awareness about the dangers of organized crime and its impact on communities and the environment. Encourage citizens to be vigilant and report suspicious activities.

9. Strengthening Legal Systems

- **Expedited Trials**: Implement expedited trial processes for cases involving organized crime to minimize delays and ensure justice is served swiftly.

- **Anti-Corruption Measures**: Strengthen anti-corruption measures within legal and judicial systems to prevent criminals from manipulating the justice system.

10. Rehabilitation and Reintegration

- **Rehabilitation Programs**: Develop rehabilitation and reintegration programs for individuals who have been involved in organized crime, focusing on providing them with skills and opportunities to reintegrate into society.

Combating organized crime is an ongoing endeavor that requires adaptability and persistence. These strategies, when implemented comprehensively and in coordination with one another, can contribute to dismantling criminal networks, reducing their influence, and ensuring the safety and well-being of communities and society as a whole.

Section 8: Belief Systems and the Environment

Explore how belief systems and religions have shaped human behavior toward the environment.

Belief systems and religions have played a significant role in shaping human behavior, values, and attitudes toward the environment. This section delves into the complex relationship between belief systems and environmental perspectives, examining how various faiths, including Christianity, Islam, Judaism, Buddhism, Hinduism, and Shamanism, have influenced human interactions with the natural world.

1. The Influence of Religious Teachings

- **Sacred Texts**: Explore the teachings found in the sacred texts of major world religions, such as the Bible in Christianity, the Quran in Islam, the Torah in Judaism, and scriptures in Buddhism and Hinduism, regarding the environment. Analyze passages that emphasize stewardship, responsibility, and care for the Earth.

- **Creation Stories**: Examine creation narratives within different belief systems and how they frame humanity's place in the natural order. Discuss interpretations that emphasize harmony with nature versus dominion over it.

- **Shamanic Perspectives**: Investigate the spiritual beliefs of Shamanism, which often emphasize the interconnectedness of all living beings and the sacredness of the natural world. Explore how Shamans serve as mediators between the human and spirit realms, fostering a deep reverence for nature.

- In Christianity, the Bible contains passages that emphasize stewardship and responsibility for the Earth. For example, Genesis 2:15 states, "The Lord God took the man and put him in the Garden of Eden to work it and take care of it."

- In Islam, the Quran calls for responsible stewardship of the Earth. Surah Al-An'am (6:141) mentions, "And He it is who produces gardens trellised and untrellised, and date palms, and crops of different shape and taste (its fruits and its provisions) and olives, and pomegranates, similar (in kind) and different (in taste)."

- Judaism's Torah emphasizes the concept of "bal tashchit," which means "do not destroy." Deuteronomy 20:19-20 instructs, "When you besiege a city for a long time, making war against it to take it, you shall not destroy its trees by wielding an axe against them."

Creation Stories:

- Christianity: In the Christian creation narrative, God places Adam and Eve in the Garden of Eden, highlighting the harmony between humanity and nature before the fall.

- Hinduism: Hindu creation stories, like the Purusha Sukta, emphasize the interconnectedness of all living beings, promoting a sense of unity and responsibility toward nature.

- Indigenous Shamanic beliefs: Shamans often recount creation stories that depict nature and its elements as sacred. These stories emphasize humanity's role as caretakers of the Earth, reinforcing a reverence for the natural world.

Shamanic Perspectives:

- Shamanism embraces the idea of the interconnectedness of all life forms. Shamans believe in communicating with spirits and nature entities to maintain balance in the ecosystem.

- Examples include rituals where Shamans seek guidance from natural elements like trees, rivers, and animals, viewing them as sacred messengers. These rituals promote a deep connection with nature and reinforce the responsibility to protect it.

- Shamanic practices like "vision quests" involve individuals spending time alone in the wilderness to connect with the natural world and gain insights into their role in preserving it.

This comprehensive approach highlights how different belief systems, including Christianity, Islam, Judaism, Hinduism, and Shamanism, offer diverse perspectives on humanity's relationship with the environment, from sacred texts and creation narratives to the interconnectedness of all living beings. These examples illustrate the various ways in which religious teachings influence environmental attitudes and behaviors.

2. Historical Practices and Rituals

- **Cultural Practices**: Investigate historical practices and rituals associated with various belief systems and their ecological implications. For example, rituals related to agriculture, hunting, and resource management.

- **Sustainability and Conservation**: Highlight examples of religious communities that have embraced sustainable and conservation-focused practices in response to their spiritual beliefs, including indigenous and Shamanic traditions.

- In Hinduism, the festival of Makar Sankranti involves flying kites. This tradition has an ecological aspect as it marks the transition of the sun into the northern hemisphere, symbolizing the harvest season and the need for balance in nature.

- Native American tribes had ceremonies like the "Buffalo Dance" as an expression of gratitude for the buffalo, their primary source of sustenance. These rituals underscored the importance of sustainable hunting practices and the interdependence of humans and nature.

- In ancient Greece, the Eleusinian Mysteries were celebrated in honor of Demeter, the goddess of agriculture. These rituals emphasized the sanctity of the Earth and the cyclical nature of life, fostering agricultural sustainability.

Sustainability and Conservation:

- Jainism, an ancient Indian religion, promotes non-violence (ahimsa) and compassion for all living beings. Jain monks sweep the ground before them to avoid stepping on insects, and they are known for their strict vegetarianism, emphasizing the conservation of life.

- Indigenous communities in the Amazon rainforest have long practiced sustainable agriculture, known as "swidden" or "slash-and-burn" farming. This method involves rotating cultivation areas, allowing the land to recover and maintain biodiversity.

- In Shamanic traditions, rituals are often centered around respecting the balance of nature. For instance, before hunting, indigenous peoples may perform ceremonies to ask for permission from the spirits of the animals and to express gratitude for their sacrifice.

These examples illustrate how cultural practices and rituals within different belief systems have historically contributed to ecological sustainability and conservation. They emphasize the harmony between human activities and the environment, reinforcing the idea that spiritual beliefs can drive responsible and sustainable interactions with nature.

3. Modern Interpretations and Environmentalism

- **Environmental Movements**: Discuss the emergence of religious environmental movements and organizations that advocate for ecotheology and eco-justice within Christianity, Islam, Judaism, and other faiths. Explore how these movements integrate ecological concerns into religious practice.

- **Interfaith Dialogue**: Examine the role of interfaith dialogue in promoting environmental awareness and cooperation among diverse religious communities, including Shamans and indigenous practitioners.

- In Christianity, the "Creation Care" movement emphasizes stewardship of the Earth based on verses like Genesis 1:28, which instructs humanity to "fill the earth and subdue it." This movement has led to initiatives like the "Green Church" program, encouraging eco-friendly practices in congregations.

- Within Islam, organizations like the Islamic Foundation for Ecology and Environmental Sciences (IFEES) promote ecotheology, aligning Islamic teachings with environmental stewardship. Quranic verses such as Surah Al-An'am (6:141) are cited to advocate for responsible resource use.

- Judaism's eco-justice movement draws from verses like Deuteronomy 20:19-20, emphasizing "bal tashchit" or "do not destroy." Jewish communities have established eco-synagogues and eco-kashrut (eco-friendly kosher) practices.

- Indigenous and Shamanic communities often emphasize their spiritual connection to the land. Indigenous-led environmental movements like the Standing Rock protests highlight the intersection of spirituality and environmental activism.

Interfaith Dialogue:

- The Parliament of the World's Religions convenes leaders from diverse faiths, including Christianity, Islam, Judaism, Hinduism, Buddhism, and indigenous traditions, to discuss environmental challenges and solutions.

- The United Religions Initiative (URI) promotes cooperation among people of different faiths and spiritual traditions. URI's Environmental Network focuses on ecological sustainability and fosters interfaith understanding.

- The Indigenous and Earth-Based Spirituality Task Force, part of the Parliament of the World's Religions, brings together indigenous and Shamanic practitioners to share traditional ecological knowledge and promote environmental conservation.

These examples highlight how modern interpretations of religious teachings have given rise to environmental movements and interfaith dialogue. Such initiatives seek to address environmental challenges collectively and integrate ecological concerns into religious practices, reflecting an evolving understanding of humanity's responsibility toward the environment.

4. Ethical Frameworks and Values

- **Ethical Principles**: Explore the ethical frameworks and values provided by belief systems and religions for addressing contemporary environmental issues. Discuss concepts of responsibility, compassion, and interdependence in Christianity, Islam, Judaism, Buddhism, Hinduism, and Shamanism.

- **Conflict and Harmony**: Analyze instances where belief systems have both contributed to environmental conflicts and fostered harmony between different groups regarding resource use and conservation.

- In Christianity, the concept of "stewardship" emphasizes the responsibility of humans to care for God's creation. Verses like Psalm 24:1 state, "The earth is the Lord's, and everything in it." This underscores the idea of humans as caretakers of the Earth.

- Islam's principles of "amanah" (trust) and "khilafah" (stewardship) stress the ethical responsibility to protect and preserve the Earth. Surah Ar-Rum (30:41) mentions, "Corruption has appeared throughout the land and sea by [reason of] what the hands of people have earned so He [i.e., Allah] may let them taste part of [the consequence of] what they have done that perhaps they will return [to righteousness]."

- Judaism's ethical values include "tikkun olam," which means "repairing the world." This concept underscores the Jewish commitment to heal and restore the world through ethical action and social justice.

- Buddhism's teachings on interconnectedness (dependent origination) emphasize that all beings are interconnected, and actions should be guided by compassion. Buddha's words in the Dhammapada state, "All tremble at violence; all fear death. Putting oneself in the place of another, one should not kill nor cause another to kill."

- Hinduism promotes "ahimsa" (non-violence) as a central ethical principle. The Bhagavad Gita (Chapter 16, Verse 2) states, "Non-violence, truth, freedom from anger, renunciation, tranquility, restraint from fault-finding, compassion for all creatures, absence of haughtiness."

Shamanism's Ethical Values:

- Shamanism emphasizes the interconnectedness of all life forms and the sacredness of the natural world. Ethical values include a deep reverence for nature, a sense of responsibility in maintaining balance, and the belief that harming the environment harms oneself.

These ethical frameworks and values provide guidance for believers in addressing contemporary environmental issues. They emphasize concepts of responsibility, compassion, and interdependence, encouraging individuals from various faiths to take ethical action for the protection and preservation of the Earth.

5. Challenges and Controversies

- **Religious Opposition**: Address instances where religious beliefs have been used to oppose environmental conservation efforts, such as debates over land use, resource extraction, or climate change denial, across various faiths and Shamanic traditions.

- **Intersections with Science**: Discuss how belief systems intersect with scientific understanding of the environment and explore areas of convergence and conflict within Christianity, Islam, Judaism, Buddhism, Hinduism, and Shamanism.

Religious Opposition:

- In Christianity, debates have arisen over climate change denial, with some religious groups opposing climate science findings, citing biblical interpretations that downplay human impact on the environment.

- In certain Islamic communities, there has been resistance to environmental conservation efforts that are seen as conflicting with traditional practices, such as deforestation in the name of expanding agriculture.

- Judaism has experienced controversies regarding land use, particularly in the context of Israeli settlements in disputed territories, which involve environmental concerns.

- Some Buddhist traditions have faced opposition to wildlife conservation efforts, where practices like the use of animal parts in traditional medicine conflict with conservation principles.

- Hinduism's diverse practices can sometimes involve environmental harm, such as rituals involving animal sacrifices or pollution of sacred rivers.

Intersections with Science:

- Within Christianity, there are areas of convergence with science, particularly among denominations that embrace ecological theology and support climate science. However, conflicts persist in areas where scientific findings challenge traditional interpretations.

- Islamic scholars have engaged in ecotheology discussions and embraced science in areas like astronomy and medicine. However, there can be tensions when science and religious interpretations clash.

- Jewish scholars have explored environmental ethics and found convergence with ecological science. The Jewish concept of "tikkun olam" aligns with efforts to address ecological challenges.

- Buddhism, with its emphasis on compassion and interconnectedness, often aligns with ecological and scientific understanding. However, conflicts may arise in certain practices.

- Hinduism's complex belief system intersects with various scientific disciplines. Some aspects, like reverence for the Ganges River, align with environmental concerns, while others, like rituals involving fire and animal sacrifice, may conflict with ecological principles.

These challenges and controversies underscore the complexity of aligning religious beliefs with environmental conservation efforts. While some faiths have made efforts to reconcile their beliefs with scientific understanding, conflicts and oppositions persist in various contexts. Balancing faith, tradition, and ecological concerns remains an ongoing challenge.

6. The Role of Indigenous and Traditional Beliefs

- **Indigenous Knowledge**: Highlight the significance of indigenous and traditional belief systems, including Shamanism, in preserving biodiversity and sustainable resource management. Explore the wisdom of indigenous communities in maintaining ecological balance.

- **Cultural Heritage**: Discuss the importance of preserving indigenous and Shamanic cultural heritage as a means of safeguarding unique environmental knowledge and practices.

Indigenous Knowledge:

- Indigenous communities, including those practicing Shamanism, possess valuable ecological knowledge that has been passed down through generations. This knowledge often includes insights into local flora, fauna, and ecosystems, as well as sustainable resource management practices.

- For example, many indigenous cultures have deep ecological wisdom about the medicinal properties of local plants and how to harvest them sustainably without harming the environment.

Cultural Heritage:

- Preserving indigenous and Shamanic cultural heritage is essential not only for the communities themselves but also for the broader world. These cultures often hold unique environmental knowledge and practices that can contribute to global conservation efforts.

- Indigenous ceremonies and rituals often center around ecological themes, reinforcing the sacredness of nature. These practices can instill a deep sense of responsibility for environmental stewardship.

- For instance, the preservation of indigenous languages is crucial, as they often contain rich vocabularies for describing the natural world and its intricate relationships.

Examples of Indigenous and Shamanic Practices:

- Indigenous tribes in the Amazon rainforest have developed sustainable methods for cultivating and harvesting crops like yams and manioc while preserving the biodiversity of the region.

- Shamanic traditions in Siberia emphasize a harmonious relationship with nature, often involving rituals to communicate with and seek guidance from spirits of the natural world.

- Native American cultures have sacred rituals and dances that celebrate the seasonal cycles and the interconnectedness of all life.

Verses and Sayings:

- Indigenous cultures often have oral traditions that include stories, sayings, and verses that emphasize the sacredness of the land and the interconnectedness of all living beings.

- A common theme in many indigenous traditions is the idea that humans are not separate from nature but an integral part of it. This perspective is reflected in their oral traditions and teachings.

Highlighting the role of indigenous and traditional belief systems, along with Shamanism, in preserving biodiversity and sustainable resource management underscores the importance of respecting and learning from these cultures. Their wisdom can contribute significantly to global efforts to protect and sustain the environment.

7. Future Perspectives and Collaboration

- **Climate Action**: Explore how belief systems can contribute to global efforts to combat climate change within Christianity, Islam, Judaism, Buddhism, Hinduism, and Shamanism. Discuss initiatives that bring together faith-based organizations, indigenous leaders, and Shamans to address urgent ecological challenges.

- **Education and Awareness**: Examine the role of religious institutions, indigenous communities, and Shamanic practices in promoting environmental education and awareness among their members and communities.

Climate Action:

- Within Christianity, various denominations have launched ecotheological initiatives that emphasize environmental stewardship and climate action. Pope Francis's encyclical "Laudato si'" highlights the Catholic Church's commitment to addressing environmental issues.

- Islamic scholars and organizations have increasingly engaged with ecological concerns. They emphasize the Quran's teachings on stewardship and responsibility, advocating for sustainable practices.

- In Judaism, environmental organizations like Hazon promote eco-Judaism, integrating ecological awareness and action into Jewish life. Tikkun olam, the principle of repairing the world, aligns with environmental efforts.

- Buddhist monks and organizations have taken part in tree planting and conservation projects. The Buddhist concept of interconnectedness underpins their commitment to environmental protection.

- Hinduism's reverence for nature is reflected in initiatives like the "Green Temples" project in India, promoting eco-friendly practices in temples and communities.

- Indigenous leaders and Shamans have increasingly collaborated with environmental organizations and scientists to address urgent ecological challenges. They bring unique insights and traditional knowledge to conservation efforts.

Education and Awareness:

- Religious institutions play a vital role in promoting environmental education and awareness among their members. Many offer programs, seminars, and publications on ecological topics.

- Indigenous communities often incorporate environmental education into their cultural teachings, ensuring that younger generations understand the importance of preserving their natural surroundings.

- Shamanic practices often involve rituals that celebrate nature and teach respect for the environment, contributing to environmental awareness among their practitioners.

Verses and Sayings:

- In Christianity, "Creation Care" movements draw inspiration from verses like Genesis 2:15, which emphasizes humanity's role as stewards of the Earth.

- In Islam, Quranic verses such as 6:141 emphasize the principle of avoiding wastefulness and consuming resources responsibly.

- Judaism's teachings include verses like Deuteronomy 20:19-20, which advocate for the preservation of fruit trees during times of conflict, reflecting ecological ethics.

- Buddhism's emphasis on compassion and interconnectedness aligns with teachings that encourage respect for all living beings and the environment.

- Hinduism's reverence for the Ganges River is reflected in verses like "Ganga Ashtakam," which praise the sacred river and call for its protection.

- Indigenous oral traditions often include stories and sayings that convey the interconnectedness of all life and the need for harmony with nature.

The future holds promising collaborations between belief systems, indigenous knowledge, and environmental efforts. These collaborations can contribute significantly to addressing ecological challenges and fostering a more sustainable and harmonious relationship with the Earth.

This comprehensive exploration of belief systems and their environmental perspectives, including the inclusion of Judaism and Shamanism, aims to foster a deeper understanding of the diverse ways in which faith-based and indigenous beliefs shape our relationship with the natural world across the spectrum of human spirituality and tradition.

Analyze teachings and doctrines related to environmental stewardship.

Within various belief systems, there are profound teachings and doctrines that emphasize the importance of environmental stewardship. These teachings often provide a moral and ethical framework for caring for the Earth and its ecosystems. By delving into these teachings, we gain valuable insights into how different religions and traditions approach the responsibility of safeguarding the environment:

Christianity:

- Christianity emphasizes the concept of humans as stewards of God's creation. This stewardship is rooted in the Bible's Book of Genesis, which describes humanity's role in taking care of the Earth. This concept encourages responsible care for the environment and cherishing the Earth as a gift from God.

Islam:

- In Islam, the Quran contains verses that highlight the balance and harmony in creation. These verses emphasize the duty of humans to act as stewards (khalifah) of the Earth, maintaining its equilibrium and preserving its resources. Islamic teachings underscore conservation and responsible use of natural resources.

Judaism:

- Judaism's teachings include principles of responsible resource management. The concept of "bal tashchit" prohibits unnecessary destruction and waste, emphasizing the ethical imperative to protect and conserve the environment.

Buddhism:

- Buddhism promotes a deep reverence for all living beings and the environment. The concept of interconnectedness underscores the importance of treating the Earth with care and compassion. This perspective encourages followers to minimize harm and act as responsible custodians of the natural world.

Hinduism:

- Hinduism's reverence for nature is reflected in the belief in the divinity of the natural world. The interconnectedness of all life is a central theme, emphasizing the need for responsible stewardship and harmonious coexistence with nature.

Indigenous and Shamanic Traditions:

- Indigenous and Shamanic traditions often view the natural world as sacred and interconnected. Their teachings stress living in harmony with nature, respecting the Earth's rhythms, and acknowledging the spiritual significance of the environment.

By analyzing these teachings and doctrines, we gain a deeper understanding of the moral and ethical foundations that guide environmental stewardship within different belief systems. These principles can serve as sources of inspiration and guidance for individuals and communities seeking to address environmental challenges.

Discuss the role of faith-based organizations in conservation efforts.

Faith-based organizations play a vital role in global conservation efforts, leveraging their moral authority, community networks, and shared values to promote environmental protection and sustainability. Here, we delve into the multifaceted role of these organizations in safeguarding the Earth:

1. **Moral Leadership:**

    - Faith-based organizations often provide moral leadership on environmental issues by emphasizing the ethical and spiritual dimensions of conservation.

    - They remind their followers of the sacredness of creation and the moral duty to protect the environment.

    - Moral guidance from religious leaders and institutions can inspire individuals and communities to take action in defense of the Earth.

2. **Advocacy and Education:**

   - Many faith-based organizations engage in advocacy efforts to influence policy and promote environmentally responsible practices.

   - They raise awareness about critical environmental issues within their congregations and beyond, encouraging responsible behavior and lifestyle choices.

   - Educational programs, workshops, and sermons often incorporate environmental themes and teachings.

3. **Environmental Stewardship Projects:**

   - Faith-based organizations initiate and participate in a wide range of environmental stewardship projects.

   - These projects may include tree planting initiatives, wildlife conservation efforts, clean energy adoption, and sustainable agriculture practices.

   - By leading by example, faith-based organizations demonstrate practical ways to care for the environment.

4. **Interfaith Collaboration:**

- Many environmental challenges are global in nature, and faith-based organizations recognize the importance of collaboration across religious boundaries.

- Interfaith dialogues and partnerships bring together diverse religious communities to address shared environmental concerns.

- These collaborations foster a sense of unity and shared responsibility for the planet.

5. **Environmental Advocacy Campaigns:**

- Faith-based organizations often launch advocacy campaigns to address specific environmental issues.

- These campaigns may focus on issues like climate change mitigation, wildlife protection, or clean water access.

- The moral authority of religious leaders can influence policymakers and galvanize public support.

6. **Community Engagement:**

- Faith-based organizations have a strong presence in communities, making them effective agents of change at the grassroots level.

- They mobilize their congregations to participate in clean-up events, conservation projects, and sustainability initiatives.

- Local engagement fosters a sense of responsibility for the environment in individual believers.

7. **Creation Care Theology:**

- Some faith-based organizations adopt creation care theology, which integrates environmental stewardship into religious doctrine.

- This theology emphasizes that caring for the Earth is an integral part of faith and reflects a broader understanding of spirituality.

- It guides believers to live in harmony with nature and consider the environmental impact of their actions.

By actively participating in conservation efforts, faith-based organizations contribute to the broader movement for environmental sustainability and offer hope for a more conscientious and responsible approach to caring for the planet.

Why We Continue to Destroy Earth even belief systems against?

The coexistence of belief systems, holy texts, and teachings that emphasize the importance of environmental protection, nonviolence, and compassion with the ongoing degradation of our planet is a complex and multifaceted issue. While religious and spiritual traditions provide ethical and moral frameworks for responsible stewardship of the Earth and peaceful coexistence, the challenges our planet faces today are influenced by a combination of factors, including economic, political, and social dynamics.

Environmental Challenges:

1. **Global Warming and Climate Change:** One of the most pressing environmental issues is global warming. The increase in greenhouse gas emissions from human activities, such as burning fossil fuels and deforestation, has led to rising global temperatures. This phenomenon disrupts weather patterns, causes more frequent and severe natural disasters, and threatens ecosystems and biodiversity.

2. **Resource Depletion:** The unsustainable extraction of natural resources, including minerals, freshwater, and forests, has strained the planet's capacity to regenerate these resources. This leads

to resource scarcity, which can result in conflicts and economic instability.

3. **Loss of Biodiversity:** Habitat destruction, pollution, and overexploitation of natural resources have led to a dramatic loss of biodiversity. Species are going extinct at an alarming rate, disrupting ecosystems and diminishing the planet's resilience to environmental changes.

4. **Pollution:** Pollution from industrial, agricultural, and urban activities contaminates air, water, and soil. It poses serious health risks to both humans and wildlife and contributes to environmental degradation.

5. **Deforestation:** The clearing of forests for agriculture, urbanization, and logging not only reduces the planet's capacity to absorb carbon dioxide but also destroys vital habitats for countless species.

Why Environmental Challenges Persist:

1. **Economic Interests:** Economic interests often clash with environmental protection. Industries that profit from activities harmful to the environment may resist regulations that would curtail their operations. The pursuit of short-term economic gains can override long-term environmental sustainability.

2. **Political Factors:** Environmental policies and international agreements are influenced by political dynamics. Some governments may prioritize economic development over environmental conservation, while global cooperation on environmental issues can be hindered by geopolitical tensions.

3. **Consumerism:** Consumer culture and the demand for goods and services have led to resource-intensive production and consumption patterns. The constant pursuit of more material possessions contributes to resource depletion and environmental degradation.

4. **Population Growth:** The global population continues to grow, placing additional stress on natural resources and ecosystems. The challenges of providing food, clean water, and energy for a growing population exacerbate environmental issues.

Belief Systems and Environmental Protection:

While belief systems, holy texts, and spiritual teachings provide ethical guidance for environmental stewardship, the application of these principles can vary widely among individuals and communities. Some adherents actively incorporate ecological responsibility into their faith practice, while others may prioritize other aspects of their beliefs or may not be aware of the environmental teachings within their religion.

Quantifying Belief in Environmental Values:

It is challenging to quantify precisely how many people worldwide adhere to belief systems that advocate for environmental protection. Additionally, belief systems are diverse, and interpretations of religious texts can vary among individuals and denominations. Therefore, it's difficult to provide an exact percentage of the global population that actively integrates environmental values into their belief system.

Promoting Environmental Change:

Despite the challenges, there are efforts worldwide to promote environmental change through faith-based organizations, interfaith dialogues, and grassroots movements. These initiatives aim to raise awareness, advocate for policy changes, and inspire individual and collective action to address environmental issues.

In conclusion, while belief systems and holy texts advocate for environmental protection and nonviolence, addressing the complex and interconnected environmental challenges our planet faces requires a multifaceted approach. This includes changes in economic systems, political will, sustainable consumption patterns, and global cooperation. The coalescence of these efforts, guided by ethical principles and the wisdom of belief systems, can contribute to a more sustainable and harmonious future for our planet.

Believers in Our Planet

Some estimated figures for the global distribution of major religious groups. These figures are approximate and can change over time due to various factors, including population growth, conversion, and other demographic trends. For the most current and accurate data, it's advisable to consult reputable sources and research organizations that specialize in religious demographics. (Source: Wikipedia)

1. Christianity: Approximately 31.7% of the global population.

2. Islam: Approximately 25% of the global population.

3. Secular/Atheist/Agnostic/Non-religious: Approximately 15.2% of the global population.

4. Hinduism: Approximately 14.9% of the global population.

5. Buddhism: Approximately 6.6% of the global population.

6. Judaism: Approximately 0.3% of the global population.

7. Other Religions (including traditional, indigenous, and folk religions): Approximately 6.3% of the global population.

So, based on these estimates, approximately 85.7% of the global population identifies as believers in one of the major religions or belief systems.

Conclusion of Chapter 1:

In this chapter, we embarked on a journey through Earth's history, exploring its cosmic context within the Milky Way galaxy and the significant events that have shaped its course. We delved into the human story, examining population growth, environmental challenges, and the impacts of wars, conflicts, and other human actions on our planet.

Throughout our exploration, we've uncovered several key insights:

1. Earth's Cosmic Address: Our home planet resides within the vast Milky Way galaxy, a remarkable cosmic system comprising billions of stars and planets. Understanding our place in this grand scheme underscores the importance of preserving the unique biosphere we call home.

2. Human Population Dynamics: The human population has experienced exponential growth,

leading to profound consequences for resource consumption, environmental degradation, and societal challenges. The Agricultural and Industrial Revolutions were pivotal milestones in this journey.

3. Environmental Impact: Population growth has transformed Earth's landscapes, strained its resources, and contributed to issues like resource scarcity, climate change, and loss of biodiversity. These challenges are interconnected and require comprehensive solutions.

4. Wars and Conflicts: Throughout history, wars and conflicts have left enduring scars on both human societies and the environment. The consequences of armed conflicts include destruction of ecosystems, displacement of communities, and lasting trauma.

5. Lessons from the Past: Earth's history serves as a crucial guide for understanding the interconnectedness of human actions and their environmental repercussions. Learning from the past is essential to preventing further destruction.

As we move forward in our exploration of the challenges and opportunities facing our planet, it is clear that the lessons from Earth's history will continue to inform our actions and decisions. The journey has just begun, and the path ahead holds both challenges and the potential for positive change.

Reinforce the importance of learning from the past to guide future actions.

In the course of our examination of Earth's history, one recurring theme has emerged as a guiding principle for our future endeavors: the vital importance of learning from the past. Our journey through the annals of time has revealed the profound impact that human actions and choices have had on our planet, both for better and for worse.

The lessons we extract from the pages of history are invaluable. They provide us with insights into the consequences of unchecked population growth, the ravages of armed conflicts, and the deep-rooted connections between environmental health and human well-being. By reflecting on the triumphs and failures of our past, we gain a clearer understanding of the paths we must tread and the pitfalls we must avoid.

As we look to the future, the imperative to apply these lessons becomes clear. We stand at a critical juncture in the history of our planet, where the challenges of resource scarcity, environmental degradation, and global cooperation loom large. To navigate these challenges successfully, we must heed the warnings and embrace the wisdom embedded in Earth's history.

In doing so, we acknowledge that our actions today will shape the world of tomorrow. We recognize that sustainable practices, responsible stewardship of our environment, and a commitment to peace are not just lofty ideals; they are prerequisites for a thriving and harmonious future. By learning from the past, we can forge a path toward a world where our planet is safeguarded, and the mistakes of yesteryears do not become the legacy of generations to come.

Let us, therefore, carry forward the knowledge gained from Earth's history as a torch that lights our way toward a more sustainable, equitable, and compassionate world. The past is our teacher, and the future is our canvas. It is within our power to paint a masterpiece, one that honors the lessons of yesterday and leaves a legacy of hope and resilience for the generations yet to come.

Transition to the next chapter, highlighting the need for proactive measures to safeguard the planet's future.

As we close the chapter on Earth's history, we stand at a crossroads where the choices we make will reverberate through time. The narrative of our past has illuminated the challenges we face today, but it has also illuminated the path forward—a path that demands our attention, dedication, and collective action.

In the forthcoming chapter, we will delve into the intricacies of our current global landscape, where the population burgeons, resources dwindle, and the environment bears the scars of our actions. Yet, it is a chapter that also holds the promise of innovation, cooperation, and transformation.

We will explore the trajectories of population growth, the complexities of food and water security, the ever-evolving state of our environment, and the profound impact of belief systems on our relationship with the Earth. Throughout our journey, one overarching theme will persist: the imperative for proactive measures.

The time for action is now. We have the knowledge, the tools, and the capacity to shape a future where the destructive patterns of the past are replaced with sustainable, harmonious coexistence. It is a future where Earth's natural wonders are cherished, where all people have access to the essentials of life, and where the bonds of peace and understanding transcend divisions.

As we embark on this next chapter, let us do so with a commitment to safeguarding our planet's future. Let us recognize that our collective responsibility to Earth is not a burden but an opportunity—an opportunity to leave a legacy of resilience, compassion, and environmental stewardship for generations to come. Join us in this vital exploration, as we seek the path to a brighter, more sustainable future for our planet.

Chapter 2: The Present and Future of Earth's Population

Section 1: Current World Population

In this section, we embark on a journey into the heart of our planet's most dynamic and ever-changing element—its population. The present and future of Earth's population are central to understanding the challenges and opportunities that lie ahead. Our exploration begins with a detailed examination of the current world population.

The Global Headcount

As of the most recent estimates available, the world's population stands at approximately 7.9 billion individuals, a figure that continues to climb steadily. However, this number is not just a statistical data point; it represents the incredible complexity and diversity of human life on our planet.

A Tapestry of Humanity

Imagine this global population as a grand tapestry, woven together by billions of unique threads. Each thread represents an individual life, a story, a family, and a community. Within this tapestry, you'll find an astonishing array of cultures, languages, and traditions.

Cultural Diversity

Around the world, there are thousands of distinct cultures, each with its own customs, practices, and worldviews. From the vibrant celebrations of Diwali in India to the intricate tea ceremonies of Japan, from the rhythmic dances of Africa to the solemn rituals of indigenous tribes in the Amazon rainforest, the diversity of human culture is awe-inspiring.

Linguistic Richness

Languages are the vessels of culture and identity. There are over 7,000 languages spoken on Earth, reflecting the vast linguistic diversity of our species. From the lyrical tones of Mandarin Chinese to the intricate grammar of Finnish, languages are not just tools for communication but also repositories of history, knowledge, and heritage.

Belief Systems

Within this global population, a multitude of belief systems flourish. Major world religions like Christianity, Islam, Hinduism, Buddhism, and Judaism, as well as countless indigenous and folk belief systems, provide spiritual and moral guidance to individuals and communities. These belief systems shape values, ethics, and perspectives on the environment and our role in it.

Aspirations and Dreams

Behind each individual in this global headcount, there are aspirations, dreams, and goals. People aspire to live in peace, provide for their families, pursue education, seek happiness, and contribute to their communities. These shared human desires transcend borders and languages, connecting us all as members of the same global family.

Challenges and Opportunities

While the sheer size and diversity of our global population are sources of wonder, they also present unique challenges and opportunities. Providing education, healthcare, and economic opportunities for billions of people is a monumental task. However, it also means that we have a vast pool of knowledge, creativity, and innovation to draw from as we address global challenges.

In Conclusion

Understanding the global headcount is not just about numbers; it's about recognizing the richness of human experience and the interconnectedness of our world. As we explore the present and future of Earth's population in this chapter, we will uncover the complexities and dynamics that define our global society. From demographic trends to cultural shifts, we will unravel the story of humanity in the 21st century.

Population Distribution

But where do these billions of people reside? The distribution of the global population is far from uniform. While some regions teem with humanity, others remain sparsely populated. As we delve into this section, we'll explore the uneven distribution of people across the continents and nations, shedding light on the factors that drive these disparities.

Continental Variances

When we examine the distribution of the global population at the continental level, striking disparities emerge. Asia, the largest continent by land area, also hosts the largest share of the world's population. With nations like China and India each boasting over a billion inhabitants, Asia is a densely populated hub of human activity.

In contrast, regions like Oceania and Antarctica have only sparse human presence. Antarctica, with its harsh climate and vast ice sheets, is inhabited by a rotating population of researchers and support staff who brave the extreme conditions in the name of scientific exploration.

Regional Clusters

Within continents, we often find regional clusters of high population density. For instance, Europe is a compact continent with numerous densely populated countries, such as Germany and the Netherlands. These regions have favorable conditions for human habitation, including arable land, temperate climates, and access to resources.

Africa, while vast and diverse, also contains areas of concentrated population, particularly in its urban centers. Cities like Lagos, Cairo, and Nairobi are vibrant, bustling metropolises where millions of people live, work, and pursue their aspirations.

Urbanization Trends

The phenomenon of urbanization plays a significant role in population distribution. Across the globe, people are increasingly drawn to cities in search of economic opportunities and improved living standards. This migration from rural to urban areas has transformed the demographic landscape, leading to the rapid growth of megacities and metropolitan regions.

Geographical Factors

Geographical features and climate are crucial determinants of population distribution. Coastal areas tend to be densely populated due to access to trade routes, transportation, and fishing. Fertile river valleys, like the Nile in Egypt and the Ganges in India, have historically supported thriving civilizations.

On the other hand, arid deserts, mountainous terrain, and dense forests often limit human settlement. These areas may have low population density due to the challenges they pose for agriculture, infrastructure development, and human habitation.

Economic and Political Factors

Economic opportunities and political stability also influence population distribution. Regions with robust economies and political stability tend to attract more residents. Conversely, areas plagued by conflict, poverty, or environmental degradation may experience population outflows.

Environmental Considerations

Environmental factors, including access to clean water, arable land, and natural resources, significantly impact where people choose to live. Climate change and its associated effects, such as sea-level rise and extreme weather events, are increasingly affecting population distribution as well.

In Conclusion

The distribution of the global population is a complex interplay of geographical, economic, political, and environmental factors. Understanding these disparities is crucial for addressing challenges related to resource allocation, urbanization, and sustainable development. As we continue our exploration of Earth's population, we will uncover how these distribution patterns shape our world today and in the future.

Urban vs. Rural: A Dynamic Divide

Another critical dimension of the world's population is the urban-rural divide. Our planet has experienced a significant shift in recent decades, with a growing trend toward urbanization. Mega-cities with populations in the tens of millions have become commonplace. But what drives this migration to urban centers, and what are the consequences for the environment and society?

The Urbanization Phenomenon

Urbanization is a global phenomenon characterized by the rapid growth of cities and the increasing concentration of the population in urban areas. This trend is driven by several interconnected factors:

1. **Economic Opportunities:** Cities often serve as economic hubs, offering diverse job opportunities in various industries. People migrate to urban areas in search of better employment prospects and higher incomes. The promise of upward mobility draws individuals from rural areas to cities.

2. **Infrastructure and Services:** Urban centers typically have better infrastructure and access to essential services such as healthcare, education, and transportation. Improved amenities and a higher standard of living can be powerful motivators for urban migration.

3. **Technological Advancements:** The digital age has transformed the nature of work. Many urban jobs are now in the tech and information sectors, attracting a tech-savvy workforce. The allure of a connected lifestyle, with access to high-speed internet and digital conveniences, pulls people toward cities.

4. **Cultural and Social Opportunities:** Cities offer diverse cultural experiences, social networks, and entertainment options. The vibrancy of urban life, with its theaters, museums, restaurants, and nightlife, appeals to those seeking a rich cultural and social milieu.

Environmental and Societal Implications

While urbanization brings opportunities, it also presents challenges and consequences for the environment and society:

1. **Environmental Impact:** Urban areas are often characterized by high energy consumption, pollution, and increased demand for resources. The concentration of people and industries can lead to air and water pollution, deforestation, and habitat destruction. Managing waste and reducing the carbon footprint are pressing concerns in urban centers.

2. **Infrastructure Strain:** Rapid urbanization can strain infrastructure, leading to congestion, inadequate housing, and overburdened public services. The demand for housing and transportation fuels construction and land-use changes, which can have cascading effects on ecosystems.

3. **Social Dynamics:** Urbanization can reshape social structures and communities. While cities offer opportunities for diversity and social mobility, they can also lead to social disparities, alienation, and challenges in providing equitable services to a diverse population.

4. **Resource Allocation:** The influx of people to cities requires careful resource allocation. Ensuring access to clean water, sanitation, and energy for all

urban residents is crucial. Sustainable urban planning and development practices are essential for addressing these challenges.

The Future of Urbanization

Urbanization is an ongoing global trend, and its pace is expected to continue. Understanding its complexities is vital for policymakers, urban planners, and communities alike. Balancing economic growth, social equity, and environmental sustainability in urban settings is a global challenge that requires innovative solutions and collaborative efforts.

In the chapters ahead, we will delve deeper into the consequences of urbanization and explore strategies for building sustainable and resilient cities in an increasingly urbanized world.

Population Growth Trends: Unraveling the Dynamics

To truly grasp the present and future of Earth's population, we must also examine the underlying trends. Population growth rates vary dramatically between regions. Some areas are experiencing rapid expansion, while others are on the brink of demographic decline. We'll dissect these trends, exploring the factors that drive them and the potential consequences.

The Dynamics of Population Growth

1. **High-Growth Regions:** Certain regions of the world continue to experience significant population growth. Sub-Saharan Africa, for example, is home to some of the world's highest birth rates. Factors contributing to high population growth in these areas include limited access to contraceptives, cultural preferences for larger families, and high fertility rates. These regions often face challenges related to providing essential services and opportunities for their growing populations.

2. **Moderate Growth Regions:** In many parts of Asia and Latin America, population growth rates have started to stabilize but remain relatively high compared to the developed world. Improved access to education and healthcare, along with changing social norms, has led to declining fertility rates in these regions. However, the legacy of past high birth rates continues to impact population size.

3. **Low-Growth Regions:** In contrast, some regions are experiencing low population growth or even population decline. This is particularly evident in parts of Europe and East Asia. Factors contributing to these trends include advanced healthcare systems, access to contraception, and economic factors such as high costs associated with raising children. Low population growth can pose

economic challenges, such as an aging workforce and potential labor shortages.

Factors Driving Population Trends

1. **Fertility Rates:** Fertility rates, the average number of children born to a woman during her lifetime, are a key driver of population growth. High fertility rates contribute to rapid population expansion, while declining fertility rates result in more moderate growth or decline. Policies and cultural norms play a significant role in shaping fertility rates.

2. **Mortality Rates:** Improvements in healthcare, sanitation, and disease prevention have led to decreased mortality rates, particularly among infants and children. Lower mortality rates contribute to population growth by increasing the number of people who reach reproductive age.

3. **Migration:** Migration patterns also influence population dynamics. Migration can offset population decline in some regions and contribute to growth in others. Economic opportunities, political stability, and social factors are among the drivers of migration.

The Consequences and Challenges

Understanding these population growth trends is essential for addressing various global challenges:

- **Resource Demands:** Rapid population growth places increased demands on essential resources such as food, water, and energy. Ensuring sustainable resource management is crucial to meet these growing demands.

- **Urbanization:** High population growth often leads to urbanization, which presents both opportunities and challenges, as discussed in the previous section. Managing urban growth sustainably is vital.

- **Environmental Impact:** Population growth is closely linked to environmental challenges, including deforestation, habitat loss, and greenhouse gas emissions. Finding ways to balance human needs with environmental conservation is a pressing concern.

- **Socioeconomic Implications:** Demographic trends also have socioeconomic implications. Aging populations in some regions can strain social welfare systems, while youth bulges in others require investments in education and job opportunities.

- **Healthcare and Education:** Meeting the healthcare and educational needs of growing populations is paramount. Access to quality healthcare and education can significantly impact population trends.

In the sections that follow, we will delve deeper into each of these aspects, exploring the regional variations in population growth, the impact on urbanization and the environment, and strategies for addressing the challenges and opportunities presented by Earth's dynamic population trends.

The Impact of Age Structure on Our World

We'll explore the age structure of the global population. The balance between young and elderly individuals has far-reaching implications for economies, healthcare systems, and social dynamics. What does the age pyramid look like, and how might it evolve in the coming decades?

The Age Pyramid: A Snapshot of Population Distribution

1. **Youthful Populations:** In some regions, particularly in parts of Sub-Saharan Africa and South Asia, the age pyramid resembles a broad-based triangle. This shape indicates a high proportion of young people in the population. High birth rates, combined with declining infant mortality, contribute to this demographic structure. These regions are experiencing what demographers refer to as a "youth bulge," which can offer a demographic dividend if harnessed through education and employment opportunities.

2. **Balanced Populations:** In other areas, such as parts of North America and Europe, the age pyramid is more balanced. There are relatively equal proportions of young, working-age, and elderly individuals. This balance often results from lower birth rates and more stable population growth. These regions tend to have well-established healthcare and social welfare systems.

3. **Aging Populations:** Some regions, notably in East Asia and parts of Europe, exhibit an aging population structure. The pyramid narrows at the base, indicating a smaller proportion of young people and a larger proportion of elderly individuals. This aging trend is driven by declining fertility rates and increased life expectancy. While it reflects progress in healthcare and living standards, it also poses challenges related to healthcare costs and pensions.

The Demographic Dividend and Challenges

Understanding the age structure is critical for several reasons:

- **Economic Impact:** Regions with a youthful population can benefit from a demographic dividend if they invest in education, healthcare, and job creation. A productive youth population can drive economic growth. However, this window of opportunity is time-limited, as these young individuals will age, and the balance will shift.

- **Healthcare Needs:** Aging populations often require more healthcare services, especially for age-related conditions. Healthcare systems must adapt to meet the demands of an older demographic.

- **Pension Systems:** An aging population can strain pension systems as a smaller working-age population supports a growing number of retirees. Policymakers must address the sustainability of pension schemes.

- **Social Dynamics:** The balance between generations influences family structures and caregiving responsibilities. Changes in age distribution can impact social norms and intergenerational relationships.

Future Age Structure: Predictions and Implications

Predicting the future age structure of the global population is complex and depends on various factors, including fertility rates, mortality rates, and migration patterns. However, demographers anticipate several trends:

- **Continued Aging:** Many regions are expected to experience further aging as fertility rates remain low and life expectancy increases. Policymakers must plan for the associated healthcare and social challenges.

- **Youth Bulges:** Some regions will continue to have large youthful populations, presenting opportunities for economic growth if investments in education and job creation are made.

- **Urbanization:** As populations shift from rural to urban areas, urban centers may have distinct age structures, with implications for urban planning and services.

In the sections that follow, we will delve into these demographic trends, exploring how they impact economies, healthcare, and social dynamics, and examining strategies for addressing the challenges and opportunities presented by the age structure of Earth's population.

The Rich Tapestry of Ethnic and Cultural Diversity

Our world's population is not only vast but also incredibly diverse. A tapestry of ethnicities, cultures, and languages weaves through the human experience. We'll delve into the richness of this diversity, examining how it shapes societies, economies, and the way we interact with our environment.

Exploring Ethnic Diversity

1. **Ethnicity and Identity:** Ethnicity plays a central role in shaping individual and group identities. It encompasses shared customs, traditions, languages, and often a sense of belonging. Across the globe, there are thousands of distinct ethnic groups, each with its own unique cultural heritage.

2. **Ethnic Conflicts:** Unfortunately, ethnic diversity can also be a source of tension and conflict. Throughout history, many conflicts and wars have had ethnic roots, often fueled by disputes over territory, resources, or political power. Understanding these dynamics is crucial for promoting peace and reconciliation.

3. **Cultural Preservation:** Ethnic diversity is a wellspring of cultural richness. Indigenous communities, in particular, are custodians of unique knowledge, traditions, and ecological wisdom. Efforts to preserve these cultures are intertwined with the conservation of biodiversity and sustainable resource management.

The Multifaceted World of Culture

1. **Cultural Expression:** Cultures express themselves through art, music, literature, dance, and cuisine. These forms of cultural expression are not only aesthetically valuable but also windows into the collective psyche of societies.

2. **Cultural Exchange:** In our interconnected world, cultures constantly interact and influence each other. The exchange of ideas, technologies, and traditions has led to cultural fusion and innovation. Globalization has accelerated this process, creating both opportunities and challenges for cultural preservation.

3. **Cultural Heritage:** Cultural heritage encompasses tangible and intangible elements that define a culture's identity. It includes historical sites, artifacts, oral traditions, and rituals. Preserving cultural heritage is vital for maintaining a sense of identity and continuity.

The Impact on Society and the Environment

1. **Social Cohesion:** Ethnic and cultural diversity can contribute to social cohesion by fostering tolerance, understanding, and the celebration of differences. However, it can also pose challenges related to discrimination and exclusion, which must be addressed.

2. **Economic Diversity:** Cultural diversity can drive economic growth through tourism, creative industries, and the exchange of goods and services. Diverse communities often bring varied skills and perspectives to the workforce, enhancing innovation.

3. **Environmental Perspectives:** Different cultures have distinct relationships with the environment.

Indigenous cultures, for instance, often have deep ecological knowledge and sustainable practices. Understanding these perspectives can inform conservation efforts and promote sustainable resource management.

The Future of Ethnic and Cultural Diversity

As the world becomes more interconnected, ethnic and cultural diversity will continue to evolve. Factors such as migration, globalization, and urbanization will shape the demographics of diverse societies. It's essential to recognize the value of this diversity and work toward inclusive, equitable societies that celebrate and preserve the cultural and ethnic tapestry of humanity.

In the following sections, we'll explore specific examples of ethnic and cultural diversity, examine how it intersects with environmental issues, and discuss strategies for promoting intercultural understanding and cooperation in our increasingly globalized world.

Socioeconomic Disparities: Shaping the Present and Future

Socioeconomic factors are powerful determinants in the complex tapestry of Earth's population dynamics. These disparities encompass access to education, healthcare, economic opportunities, and the distribution of wealth and resources. Understanding the intricate interplay of socioeconomic factors is essential for comprehending the challenges and opportunities that lie ahead for humanity.

Access to Education

1. **Educational Divide:** Across the globe, there exists a stark educational divide. Some regions boast well-established educational systems with high literacy rates, while others struggle with limited access to quality education. This divide is often rooted in economic disparities, geographic location, and systemic inequalities.

2. **Empowerment through Education:** Education is a powerful tool for empowerment. It equips individuals with knowledge and skills, enabling them to participate in the workforce, make informed decisions, and engage as active citizens. Investing in education is not only a matter of individual well-being but also a key driver of societal progress.

3. **Gender Disparities:** Gender disparities in education persist in many parts of the world. In some communities, girls face barriers to education, including cultural norms, early marriage, and limited access to schools. Bridging the gender gap in education is vital for achieving gender equality and sustainable development.

Healthcare Access

1. **Health Inequalities:** Access to healthcare services varies dramatically. While some regions benefit from advanced healthcare systems, others lack basic medical infrastructure. Disparities in healthcare access can lead to differences in life expectancy, maternal and child mortality rates, and the prevalence of preventable diseases.

2. **Public Health Challenges:** Socioeconomic disparities often intersect with public health challenges. Vulnerable populations may face higher rates of malnutrition, inadequate sanitation, and limited access to clean water. These disparities contribute to health inequities that persist across generations.

3. **Pandemic Impacts:** The COVID-19 pandemic vividly illustrated the consequences of unequal access to healthcare. Communities with limited resources and healthcare infrastructure experienced higher infection rates and greater strain on healthcare systems. Addressing these disparities in pandemic response is essential for global health security.

Economic Opportunities

1. **Income Disparities:** Economic opportunities and income disparities vary widely across the world. While some individuals enjoy access to stable jobs, economic mobility, and financial security, others

grapple with unemployment, underemployment, and poverty. Economic inequality can perpetuate social divides and hinder societal progress.

2. **Entrepreneurship and Innovation:** Encouraging entrepreneurship and innovation is a pathway to economic growth and poverty reduction. However, not all individuals have equal access to the resources and support needed to start businesses or pursue innovative ventures. Fostering an inclusive entrepreneurial ecosystem is essential for fostering economic diversity.

3. **Rural vs. Urban Disparities:** Urban areas often offer more economic opportunities than rural regions. This urban-rural divide can drive migration to cities in search of employment, leading to rapid urbanization. Understanding the implications of this trend, including its environmental impact, is critical.

The Intersection of Socioeconomic Factors

1. **Interconnected Challenges:** Socioeconomic factors are not isolated but deeply interconnected. Lack of education can limit employment prospects, leading to income disparities and reduced access to healthcare. These challenges are often compounded, making it difficult for individuals and communities to break free from cycles of poverty.

2. **Social Mobility:** The ability to improve one's socioeconomic status through education, entrepreneurship, and economic opportunities is known as social mobility. Understanding the factors that facilitate or hinder social mobility is crucial for addressing inequality and promoting inclusive societies.

3. **Policy Solutions:** Governments, civil society, and international organizations play a pivotal role in addressing socioeconomic disparities. Policy interventions, such as investments in education and healthcare, social safety nets, and job creation programs, can mitigate these disparities and promote equitable development.

As we explore the present and future of Earth's population, it is imperative to recognize the profound impact of socioeconomic factors. These disparities not only shape individual lives but also influence the resilience and adaptability of societies in the face of global challenges. Addressing these disparities is not only a moral imperative but also a strategic necessity for building a more sustainable and inclusive world.

The Road Ahead: Navigating the Current World Population

As we embark on this journey through the intricacies of the current world population, it is essential to maintain a forward-looking perspective. The road ahead is filled with both challenges and opportunities, and understanding the present is key to making informed decisions for the future. In the chapters that follow, we'll delve into projections, demographic trends, and the pressing issues that will shape the destiny of humanity in the coming decades. But before we set our sights on the future, let us thoroughly comprehend the intricate tapestry of humanity that constitutes the current world population.

Global Dynamics and Projections

1. **Population Projections:** Demographers and experts project that the global population will continue to grow, albeit at a slower pace than in the past. Estimates suggest that by mid-century, we could see a world inhabited by over 9 billion people. Understanding the factors contributing to this growth, such as fertility rates and life expectancy, will be central to our exploration.

2. **Ageing Populations:** One prominent demographic trend is the ageing of populations in many parts of the world. As birth rates decline and life expectancy increases, a larger proportion of individuals will be in the elderly age group. This shift poses unique challenges for healthcare, pensions, and intergenerational dynamics.

3. **Youth Bulge:** Conversely, some regions will continue to experience a "youth bulge" characterized by a high percentage of young people. Harnessing the potential of youth through

education, employment, and social inclusion will be vital for sustainable development and social stability.

Environmental Considerations

1. **Environmental Impact:** The size and consumption patterns of the global population have significant implications for the environment. More people mean increased resource demands, energy consumption, and waste generation. Exploring sustainable practices and resource management will be paramount.

2. **Climate Change Mitigation:** Climate change, driven by greenhouse gas emissions, is one of the most pressing challenges of our time. Understanding the link between population growth, consumption, and climate change is crucial for designing effective mitigation strategies.

Societal and Cultural Dynamics

1. **Cultural Shifts:** The current world population is witnessing shifts in cultural norms, values, and family structures. These changes influence fertility rates, gender roles, and social expectations. Examining how societies adapt to these shifts is essential.

2. **Migration Patterns:** Human migration continues to shape the distribution of populations.

Understanding the push and pull factors behind migration, as well as its economic and social impacts, will be part of our exploration.

Economic and Technological Transformations

1. **Technological Advancements:** Rapid technological advancements are altering the way we work, communicate, and access information. These innovations have far-reaching implications for employment, education, and societal organization.

2. **Economic Growth:** Economic development remains a critical factor in population dynamics. As economies grow or face challenges, they influence fertility rates, employment opportunities, and living standards.

Health and Well-being

1. **Healthcare Access:** Access to quality healthcare is a cornerstone of individual and societal well-being. Assessing disparities in healthcare access, healthcare infrastructure, and global health security will be part of our exploration.

2. **Pandemic Preparedness:** The COVID-19 pandemic has underscored the importance of pandemic preparedness and international cooperation in addressing global health crises. Examining lessons learned and strategies for future preparedness is vital.

Interconnected Global Challenges

1. **Interplay of Challenges:** It's crucial to recognize that these challenges are interconnected. Population growth, environmental sustainability, social dynamics, and technological progress are all intertwined. Our journey will delve into these complex interplays.

As we delve deeper into these topics in the chapters ahead, we'll gain a holistic understanding of the forces that shape the world's population and, by extension, the planet's future. The road ahead is marked by both opportunities to address pressing issues and challenges that demand our collective attention and action. Together, we'll navigate this intricate landscape, armed with knowledge and a commitment to building a more sustainable and equitable world for generations to come.

Section 2: Population Projections

Predict population figures for 2050, 2075, and 3000 years from now.

Population projections for 2050, 2075, and 3000 years from now based on the assumption of no major global disruptions like pandemics or large-scale wars. Please keep in mind that these projections are speculative and rely on current demographic trends. The actual future population will depend on numerous factors, many of which are unpredictable.

2050 Population Projection: Assuming a stable global environment with no major disruptions, the world's population is projected to continue growing, albeit at a slower rate compared to previous decades. Based on current birth rates and other demographic factors, the global population could reach approximately 10.2 to 11.2 billion people by 2050.

2075 Population Projection: Extending the projection to 2075, the world's population could range from 10.5 billion to 12.5 billion under the assumption of continued stability and consistent demographic trends.

3000 Population Projection: Projecting the population 3000 years into the future is highly speculative and should be taken with caution. However, assuming no major disruptions and extrapolating current trends, the global population in the year 3000 could range from 12 billion to 15 billion.

These projections are based on the assumption of stability and continued demographic trends. It's important to reiterate that the actual population figures will be influenced by a wide range of factors, including changes in fertility rates, mortality rates, migration patterns, technological advancements, and unforeseen events. Demographic forecasting over such long timeframes is inherently uncertain.

In Realistic Projections:

Predicting population figures for the distant future, such as 2075 and 3000 years from now, involves significant uncertainties and should be taken as speculative. Nevertheless, we can provide some general projections based on current demographic trends. Please keep in mind that these projections are highly speculative and should not be considered precise estimates:

2050 Population Projection: Based on current trends, the world's population is projected to continue growing, albeit at a slower rate than in previous decades. By 2050, it is estimated that the global population could reach approximately 9.7 to 10.9 billion people. However, this projection is subject to change based on factors like fertility rates, mortality rates, and migration patterns.

2075 Population Projection: Projecting population figures for 2075 becomes increasingly uncertain, and the range of possibilities widens. Depending on various demographic scenarios, the global population could range from 9 billion to over 12 billion by 2075. Factors such as advances in healthcare, changes in fertility rates, and geopolitical events will heavily influence this projection.

3000 Population Projection: Looking even further into the future, projecting the world's population for the year 3000 is highly speculative. It's essential to recognize that over such a long time frame, numerous unpredictable factors can come into play, including technological advancements, environmental changes, and societal shifts. As a purely speculative estimate, the global population in the year 3000 could range from 10 billion to 20 billion or more, depending on a multitude of unknown variables.

These projections serve as rough estimates and should not be considered definitive. Demographic forecasting is a complex field, and long-term projections are highly uncertain due to the dynamic nature of human societies and the planet itself. For precise and up-to-date population projections, it is advisable to refer to authoritative sources like the United Nations or academic research institutions that specialize in demography.

Population Projections in the Face of Uncertainty: Scenarios of Pandemics, Global Conflict, and Regional Tensions

Projections for the world's population in the scenarios of a pandemic, a third World war, and a potential conflict between China and India. Please keep in mind that these projections are speculative and based on various assumptions.

Scenario 1: Impact of a Pandemic If the world were to face a widely spread pandemic similar in scale to the COVID-19 pandemic, it could have a significant impact on population growth. In such a scenario, the global population growth rate may slow down or even temporarily decline due to increased mortality rates. Birth rates may also be affected by factors such as economic instability and changes in family planning.

- **2050 Population Projection (with Pandemic Impact):** The world's population growth could be significantly lower than the previous projection, possibly ranging from 9.5 to 10.5 billion by 2050.

- **2075 Population Projection (with Pandemic Impact):** By 2075, the global population may range from 9.8 billion to 11.8 billion, assuming recovery from the pandemic's impact.

- **3000 Population Projection (with Pandemic Impact):** Projections for the year 3000 are highly uncertain, but if a pandemic has a long-lasting impact, the global population could range from 11 billion to 14 billion.

Scenario 2: Impact of a Third World War A large-scale global conflict, such as a third World war, could have catastrophic consequences for humanity, including a significant loss of life, displacement of populations, and destruction of infrastructure. It's challenging to provide precise population projections in such a scenario due to the unpredictability of war outcomes.

- **2050 Population Projection (with Third World War Impact):** Population projections in the aftermath of a global war would be highly uncertain, but they could be significantly lower than previous estimates. The global population may range from 8 billion to 9.5 billion by 2050, depending on the extent of the conflict's impact.

- **2075 Population Projection (with Third World War Impact):** By 2075, if the world has emerged from a devastating war, the global population could range from 7 billion to 9 billion.

- **3000 Population Projection (with Third World War Impact):** Projections for the year 3000 would be even more speculative, with the global population possibly ranging from 6 billion to 8 billion, depending on the long-term consequences of the war.

Scenario 3: China-India Conflict A conflict between two highly populated countries like China and India would have significant regional and potentially global implications. However, it's important to note that providing precise population projections for this scenario is challenging due to the complex geopolitical factors involved.

- **2050 Population Projection (with China-India Conflict Impact):** In the event of a conflict between China and India, the impact on the global population would largely depend on the extent of the conflict and its consequences. Assuming a significant impact, the global population may range from 9 billion to 10.5 billion by 2050.

- **2075 Population Projection (with China-India Conflict Impact):** By 2075, if the conflict has had lasting effects, the global population could range from 9.5 billion to 11 billion.

- **3000 Population Projection (with China-India Conflict Impact):** Projections for the year 3000 would be highly uncertain, but if the conflict has long-term consequences, the global population might range from 10 billion to 12 billion.

Please remember that these projections are highly speculative, and the actual outcomes would depend on numerous unpredictable factors. These scenarios highlight the potential impacts of major global events on population growth but should not be taken as precise forecasts.

Speculations:

A nuclear conflict involving less than 3 per cent of the world's stockpiles could kill one-third of the world's population within two years, according to a new international study led by scientists at Rutgers University.

A larger nuclear conflict between Russia and the US could kill three-fourths of the world's population in the same time. (https://www.scmp.com/

A Scientific Report:

Nuclear Famine: climate effects of regional nuclear war

A nuclear war using as few as 100 weapons anywhere in the world would disrupt the global climate and agricultural production so severely that the lives of more than two billion people would be in jeopardy from mass starvation.

A landmark report, Nuclear Famine (2022), published by IPPNW summarizes the latest scientific work which shows that a so-called "limited" or "regional" nuclear war would be neither limited nor regional. A war that detonated less than 1/20th of the world's nuclear weapons would still crash the climate, the global food supply chains, and likely public order. Famines and unrest would kill hundreds of millions, perhaps even billions. The findings come at a time of greatly heightened tensions among nuclear states and amid warnings that we are closer to nuclear war than we have ever been.

Using less than 3% of the world's nuclear weapons, a nuclear war between India and Pakistan could kill up to every 3rd person on earth, with average global temperatures dropping about 1.3 degrees Celsius.

A full-scale nuclear war between the United States and Russia would kill an estimated 5 billion people worldwide within two years. (https://www.ippnw.org/).

Chapter 3: Environmental Sustainability

Section 1: Current Resource Availability

Assess whether there is enough food, clean water, and a clean environment.

In this section, we delve into the assessment of the world's current resource availability, focusing on the fundamental elements of survival: food, clean water, and a healthy environment.

The Global Food Supply

The global food supply is a dynamic and intricate web of agricultural production, distribution networks, and consumption patterns. In this section, we'll thoroughly examine the key components that constitute the state of our world's food supply.

Global Agricultural Practices: Nourishing the World

Agriculture is the lifeblood of human existence, providing sustenance for our ever-growing global population. This section delves into the diverse realm of agricultural practices, spanning centuries of wisdom and cutting-edge innovations. Here, we journey through the rich tapestry of agriculture, acknowledging traditional methods that have stood the test of time and the modern technologies promising increased yields and food security. Moreover, we touch upon the controversies surrounding agriculture, such as the use of genetically modified crops and chemical inputs, and their profound implications for sustainability.

Agriculture's Historical Significance:

From the fertile crescents of ancient Mesopotamia to the terraced rice fields of Southeast Asia, agriculture has been the bedrock of human civilization. Traditional farming practices, passed down through generations, reflect the intimate knowledge of ecosystems and the environment. They emphasize harmony with nature, showcasing humanity's profound connection to the land.

The Modern Agricultural Revolution:

The 20th century ushered in an agricultural revolution of unprecedented scale. Mechanization, synthetic fertilizers, and pesticides catapulted crop yields, heralding the era of industrial agriculture. This transformation allowed us to feed the world's booming population. However, it also raised questions about sustainability, resource depletion, and environmental impact. Today, we'll examine these innovations, recognizing both their benefits and the critical need to address their challenges.

Genetically Modified Crops:

Genetically modified organisms (GMOs) are at the forefront of agricultural debates. Engineered for traits like pest resistance or herbicide tolerance, GMOs have sparked discussions about safety, ecological effects, and long-term consequences. We'll navigate this complex terrain, exploring the science behind GMOs and the ethical, environmental, and regulatory dimensions that influence their adoption.

Chemical Inputs and Environmental Sustainability:

Chemical inputs, including synthetic fertilizers and pesticides, have become integral to modern agriculture. While they boost yields and protect crops, they also pose environmental and health concerns. We'll delve into the use of these inputs, discussing responsible practices and the urgent need for sustainable alternatives that reduce agriculture's ecological footprint.

Our journey through global agricultural practices underscores their critical role in feeding humanity. We celebrate the wisdom of traditional methods and recognize the transformative power of modern innovations. By gaining deeper insights into these practices, we empower ourselves to make informed choices that ensure food security while safeguarding the health of our planet.

Food Distribution Networks: Connecting Supply to Demand

In our exploration of food-related subjects, the intricate web of food distribution networks demands our attention. Without efficient systems to connect agricultural producers with consumers, the bounty of the harvest may never reach our plates.

The Journey of Food:

The journey of food from source to consumer is a multifaceted process, encompassing transportation, storage, and retailing. It begins at the farm, where crops are harvested and livestock raised. From there, food travels via various channels, including trucks, ships, and planes, before arriving at distribution centers and local markets.

Food distribution is a symphony of logistics and coordination. Each step in the journey requires meticulous planning to ensure that food remains fresh and safe for consumption. Storage facilities are strategically located to prevent spoilage, and refrigerated transport maintains the integrity of perishable goods.

Globalization and Food Trade:

In an increasingly interconnected world, food trade has become a global affair. Nations import and export food to meet their demands and fill gaps in supply. This globalization has both benefits and challenges, fostering diversity in food choices but also exposing vulnerabilities to disruptions.

Global food trade has led to greater food security for many regions. It allows countries to access a wider variety of food products, reducing their dependence on local production. For consumers, this means a year-round availability of fruits, vegetables, and other products that were once seasonal.

However, globalization also poses risks. Food supply chains are susceptible to various shocks, including economic downturns, climate change, and geopolitical conflicts. The COVID-19 pandemic illustrated how interconnected these systems are, with disruptions in one part of the world affecting access to goods thousands of miles away.

Challenges and Resilience:

Food distribution networks face a myriad of challenges, from ensuring perishable items remain fresh during transit to minimizing food waste. One critical challenge is the need to balance efficiency with resilience. Lean supply chains can be highly efficient but are vulnerable to disruptions. More resilient systems may have redundancies built in to withstand shocks, but they can be less efficient.

The COVID-19 pandemic tested the resilience of food distribution networks globally. Lockdowns, transportation restrictions, and panic buying led to temporary disruptions in the supply of some goods. However, the crisis also prompted innovation and adaptation. Restaurants shifted to takeout and delivery, and online grocery shopping saw a surge in popularity.

Local and Sustainable Food Movements:

Amidst the complexities of global food distribution, there is a growing movement towards local and sustainable food systems. Communities are reimagining how food reaches their tables by prioritizing nearby farms and reducing food miles. This shift emphasizes environmental sustainability, supports local economies, and fosters stronger connections between producers and consumers.

Local and sustainable food movements are driven by several key principles:

1. **Reducing Food Miles:** One of the central tenets of the movement is reducing the distance food travels from farm to table. This reduces carbon emissions associated with transportation and supports local agriculture.

2. **Supporting Local Economies:** Buying from local farmers and producers keeps money within the community and supports small-scale agriculture.

3. **Seasonal Eating:** Embracing seasonal foods reduces the need for energy-intensive greenhouse production and long-distance transportation.

4. **Sustainable Practices:** Many local and sustainable food producers prioritize environmentally friendly practices, such as organic farming, reduced pesticide use, and responsible water management.

5. **Community Building:** These movements often involve farmers' markets, community-supported agriculture (CSA) programs, and other initiatives that bring producers and consumers together.

The shift towards local and sustainable food systems is a response to concerns about the environmental impact of global food distribution and a desire for greater transparency in the food supply chain. It represents a return to some of the principles of traditional agriculture, where communities relied on local resources and knowledge.

Conclusion:

Food distribution networks are the unsung heroes of our daily sustenance. They bridge the gap between production and consumption, ensuring a diverse array of food is available to nourish our communities. By understanding the intricacies and challenges of these networks, we gain insights into how to make them more resilient, sustainable, and equitable.

The COVID-19 pandemic has highlighted the need for adaptable and resilient food distribution systems. As we look to the future, it's clear that ongoing innovation and collaboration will be essential to meet the challenges of a growing global population, changing consumption patterns, and environmental sustainability. Food distribution will remain a dynamic and vital component of our interconnected world.

Challenges of Food Security: Ensuring Everyone Is Well-Fed

In our quest to understand the current state of food security, we must confront the multifaceted challenges that threaten the availability and accessibility of safe and nutritious food for all. Food security, a fundamental human right, remains elusive for millions around the globe. Our exploration will take us through the key challenges faced by communities and nations as they strive to ensure that no one goes hungry in a world of plenty.

Economic Disparities and Food Inequality:

One of the foremost challenges to food security is economic inequality. While the world produces more than enough food to feed its entire population, the benefits of this abundance are not distributed evenly. Economic disparities limit access to food for marginalized and vulnerable populations, pushing them into a cycle of food insecurity.

For many households, a significant portion of their income is dedicated to purchasing food. When incomes are insufficient or unstable, access to an adequate diet becomes a daily struggle. Low-income families often face difficult choices between buying nutritious food and meeting other basic needs like housing and healthcare.

Food inequality also manifests in the quality and variety of available food. In economically disadvantaged areas, there may be limited access to fresh fruits and vegetables, leading to diets that are less diverse and potentially less nutritious.

Conflicts and Natural Disasters:

Conflicts and natural disasters pose acute threats to food security. Armed conflicts disrupt agricultural activities, displace communities, and damage critical infrastructure. Farmers are forced to abandon their fields, leading to reduced harvests and food shortages. Conflict zones also face challenges in delivering humanitarian aid, leaving vulnerable populations at risk of starvation.

Natural disasters, such as droughts, floods, hurricanes, and wildfires, can devastate crops and infrastructure. In regions prone to such events, communities must grapple with the aftermath, including food shortages and disrupted supply chains.

Climate Change: A Looming Threat:

Perhaps the most daunting challenge to food security is the specter of climate change. Rising global temperatures, shifting weather patterns, and extreme weather events threaten the stability of agricultural systems. Changes in temperature and precipitation can reduce crop yields and alter the geographic suitability of certain crops. Pests and diseases may thrive in warmer conditions, further jeopardizing food production.

Small-scale farmers, who comprise a significant portion of the world's agricultural workforce, are particularly vulnerable to the impacts of climate change. Many lack the resources and technology to adapt to changing conditions.

The consequences of climate change extend beyond crop yields. Sea-level rise and ocean acidification affect fisheries, disrupting the availability of fish as a food source. Climate-induced migration can strain resources in receiving areas, potentially leading to conflicts over limited food and water supplies.

Sustainable Solutions:

Addressing the challenges of food security demands a multifaceted approach. Efforts must focus on reducing economic disparities, improving the resilience of communities to conflicts and disasters, and mitigating the impacts of climate change on agriculture. Some key strategies include:

1. **Social Safety Nets:** Implementing social safety nets, such as food assistance programs and cash transfers, to support vulnerable populations during times of crisis.

2. **Climate-Resilient Agriculture:** Promoting climate-resilient agricultural practices, including drought-resistant crops and sustainable land management.

3. **Conflict Resolution:** Seeking peaceful solutions to conflicts to prevent disruption of food production and distribution.

4. **Reducing Food Waste:** Implementing measures to reduce food waste, which can help redirect surplus food to those in need.

5. **Sustainable Farming:** Encouraging sustainable and regenerative farming practices that prioritize soil health, biodiversity, and water conservation.

6. **Education and Awareness:** Raising awareness about food security issues and educating communities about sustainable food production and consumption.

The challenges of food security are complex, but they are not insurmountable. By addressing the root causes of food inequality and working together on sustainable solutions, we can move closer to a world where everyone has reliable access to the nourishment they need to thrive. Food security is not just a goal; it's a fundamental human right that we must uphold for the well-being of current and future generations.

Sustainability in Food Production: Nourishing the Planet Responsibly

In our examination of food security, it becomes evident that sustainability is the linchpin for securing a resilient global food supply. Sustainability in food production entails a fundamental shift in our agricultural practices, where the goal is not just to feed the world today but to do so in a way that preserves the Earth's capacity to feed future generations. In this section, we delve into the environmental toll of current agricultural practices and explore the urgent need for sustainable alternatives.

Current Agricultural Practices: An Unsustainable Path:

The dominant agricultural practices of the past century have enabled the world to achieve unprecedented levels of food production. However, this achievement has come at a significant cost to the environment. It's crucial to acknowledge the detrimental effects of these practices:

1. **Soil Degradation:** Intensive monoculture farming and excessive use of chemical fertilizers and pesticides have led to soil degradation. Soil erosion, loss of fertility, and compaction are common consequences. Healthy soil is the foundation of food production, and its depletion is a cause for concern.

2. **Excessive Water Usage:** Agriculture is a thirsty endeavor, accounting for a substantial portion of global freshwater consumption. In regions where water resources are scarce, excessive irrigation can deplete aquifers and lead to long-term water stress.

3. **Deforestation:** Expanding agricultural land often involves clearing forests, which not only releases stored carbon into the atmosphere but also destroys critical habitats for biodiversity. The loss

of forests contributes to climate change and disrupts ecosystems.

4. **Chemical Inputs:** The widespread use of chemical inputs, including synthetic fertilizers and pesticides, has environmental consequences. Runoff from these chemicals can pollute waterways, harming aquatic life and human health.

The Urgent Need for Transition:

The environmental toll of current agricultural practices makes it imperative to transition to sustainable and regenerative agriculture. Sustainability encompasses practices that maintain or enhance the environment's capacity to support life while meeting society's food needs. Regenerative agriculture goes a step further by aiming to restore and improve the natural resources upon which agriculture depends.

Innovative Approaches to Sustainable Agriculture:

The path to sustainable food production is paved with innovation and adaptation. By harnessing technology and ecological principles, we can reduce the environmental impact of agriculture:

1. **Precision Farming:** Precision agriculture leverages technology, such as GPS and sensors, to optimize resource use. Farmers can apply inputs

like water, fertilizers, and pesticides precisely where and when they are needed, reducing waste and environmental impact.

2. **Agroecology:** Agroecology is an ecological approach to farming that seeks to mimic natural ecosystems. By enhancing biodiversity, promoting soil health, and reducing reliance on external inputs, agroecology fosters sustainable and resilient food systems.

3. **Crop Diversity:** Diversifying crop varieties can enhance resilience to pests, diseases, and changing environmental conditions. Heirloom and locally adapted varieties may play a crucial role in building resilient food systems.

4. **Reducing Food Waste:** Addressing food waste is another facet of sustainable food production. By reducing waste at various stages of the food supply chain, we can ensure that more of what is produced reaches those in need.

A Sustainable Food Future:

In navigating the complexities of sustainability in food production, we discover that the choices we make today profoundly impact the planet's capacity to nourish us tomorrow. Sustainable agriculture is not just an option; it's a necessity for securing a resilient global food supply while safeguarding the environment. The innovations and practices discussed here offer hope that we can feed a growing population without compromising the health of our planet. As we explore further, we'll uncover additional strategies and approaches that contribute to this crucial mission of sustaining both people and the planet.

Access to Clean Water: Nurturing a Thirsty Planet

In our journey towards understanding the critical facets of environmental sustainability, we turn our attention to a fundamental element of life – clean and safe drinking water. This section delves into the availability of clean water sources, confronts the challenges posed by water scarcity, and underscores the profound significance of sustainable water management for the well-being of present and future generations.

The Precious Resource of Clean Water:

Access to clean water is not merely a convenience; it is a fundamental human right. Clean water is the lifeblood of communities, sustaining health, sanitation, and economic productivity. Unfortunately, this essential resource remains elusive for millions across the globe.

Availability of Clean Water Sources:

The availability of clean water sources varies widely, painting a stark picture of global disparities:

- **Abundant Resources:** Some regions are blessed with abundant freshwater resources, including pristine lakes, mighty rivers, and vast underground aquifers. Access to clean water is relatively unproblematic in these areas.

- **Water Stress:** Conversely, many regions grapple with water stress, where the demand for water exceeds the available supply. This situation is exacerbated by factors like population growth, climate change, and inefficient water management.

Challenges of Water Scarcity:

Water scarcity extends its reach across diverse landscapes, presenting multifaceted challenges:

1. **Human Impact:** Human activities, such as over-extraction, pollution, and mismanagement of water resources, are key drivers of water scarcity. Unsustainable agricultural practices, industrial pollution, and inadequate wastewater treatment all contribute to the problem.

2. **Climate Change:** Climate change exacerbates water scarcity by altering precipitation patterns and increasing the frequency and severity of

droughts. These changes disrupt the availability of freshwater sources.

3. **Ecological Impact:** Water scarcity not only affects humans but also jeopardizes ecosystems. Aquatic habitats suffer, aquatic species dwindle, and wetlands that provide critical ecosystem services dry up.

The Imperative of Sustainable Water Management:

Sustainable water management is the beacon that guides us through the challenges of water scarcity. It encompasses a range of practices and policies aimed at ensuring the equitable distribution of clean water while preserving the environment:

1. **Efficient Water Use:** Implementing efficient water use practices in agriculture, industry, and households can significantly reduce water demand. Technologies like drip irrigation and water-saving appliances play a crucial role.

2. **Pollution Control:** Robust measures to control water pollution, including regulations and treatment infrastructure, are essential. Preventing pollutants from entering water bodies ensures the availability of clean water.

3. **Protection of Ecosystems:** Safeguarding the health of aquatic ecosystems, such as rivers, lakes, and wetlands, is vital. Healthy ecosystems

contribute to water purification, flood control, and biodiversity conservation.

4. **Climate Resilience:** Building resilience to climate change involves adapting water management practices to changing conditions. This may include measures like the development of drought-resistant crops and improved water storage.

5. **Community Involvement:** Engaging communities in water management decisions fosters a sense of ownership and responsibility. Local knowledge and practices can contribute to sustainable solutions.

A Thirsty Planet's Hope:

Our exploration of access to clean water unveils the dire challenges faced by many and the transformative power of sustainable water management. By prioritizing clean water access, implementing conservation measures, and nurturing ecosystems, we can ensure that clean and safe drinking water remains a universally accessible human right. As we continue our journey, we'll unveil further insights and strategies that contribute to the noble mission of securing this life-sustaining resource for all.

Environmental Health and Sustainability: Nurturing Our Planet's Vital Signs

As stewards of this remarkable planet, it is our responsibility to ensure its health and sustainability for ourselves and the generations to come. In this section, we embark on a journey to explore the current state of our environment, delving into vital factors such as air and water quality, deforestation, biodiversity loss, and the pervasive impact of climate change. Through this examination, we unveil the compelling urgency for sustainable practices that will safeguard the Earth's delicate natural systems.

The State of Our Environment:

Our environment is an intricate web of interconnected systems that sustain life. It provides us with the air we breathe, the water we drink, and the resources we depend on. Yet, this complex tapestry is under duress, and understanding its current state is paramount.

Air Quality:

The air we breathe is a lifeline, but its quality varies dramatically across regions. Urban centers often grapple with air pollution, driven by industrial activities, transportation emissions, and fossil fuel combustion. The consequences of poor air quality are dire, affecting human health and contributing to climate change.

Water Quality:

Access to clean and safe drinking water is essential, yet pollution and contamination of water sources pose significant challenges. Factors such as industrial runoff, agricultural runoff laden with pesticides and fertilizers, and inadequate wastewater treatment threaten the quality of our water supply.

Deforestation:

Forests are Earth's lungs, absorbing carbon dioxide and releasing oxygen. However, deforestation, driven by logging, urban expansion, and agriculture, has far-reaching consequences. It disrupts ecosystems, reduces biodiversity, and contributes to greenhouse gas emissions.

Biodiversity Loss:

The intricate web of life on our planet is unraveling. Species are vanishing at an alarming rate due to habitat destruction, poaching, and the impacts of climate change. Biodiversity loss not only threatens ecosystems but also compromises our own food security and medicine sources.

The Impact of Climate Change:

Perhaps the most pressing environmental challenge of our time, climate change is transforming our planet. Rising temperatures, extreme weather events, sea-level rise, and disruptions to ecosystems are all manifestations of this global crisis. The consequences are profound, affecting everything from food production to human migration patterns.

The Urgency of Sustainability:

Our examination of environmental health and sustainability underscores the compelling need for transformative action:

1. **Mitigating Climate Change:** Aggressive efforts to reduce greenhouse gas emissions are essential. Transitioning to renewable energy sources, enhancing energy efficiency, and implementing climate-resilient infrastructure are key strategies.

2. **Conservation and Restoration:** Protecting natural habitats and restoring damaged ecosystems are critical for biodiversity conservation. These efforts not only preserve wildlife but also enhance resilience to environmental challenges.

3. **Cleaner Air and Water:** Implementing stringent regulations and adopting clean technologies are essential for improving air and water quality. Sustainable agriculture and responsible waste management are integral components.

4. **Global Collaboration:** Addressing environmental challenges requires international cooperation.

Agreements like the Paris Agreement on climate change serve as frameworks for collective action.

5. **Education and Advocacy:** Raising awareness and advocating for sustainable practices are instrumental in driving change. Education empowers individuals to make informed choices and demand action from policymakers.

Nurturing Our Planet's Vital Signs:

Our journey into environmental health and sustainability is a clarion call to action. It serves as a reminder of our interconnectedness with the Earth and the urgency of adopting sustainable practices. As we navigate the complex terrain of environmental challenges, we will continue to unveil insights, strategies, and examples of positive change that inspire hope for a healthier and more sustainable world.

Population and Resource Dynamics: Navigating a Complex Relationship

In our exploration of the intricate web that is Earth's sustenance, we must turn our gaze to the dynamic interplay between population growth and resource availability. This relationship is a tapestry woven with complexity, where the size and distribution of the global population intersect with the utilization of Earth's finite resources. In this section, we embark on a journey to dissect these intricate interactions, revealing the challenges and opportunities that emerge from this ever-evolving dynamic.

The Complex Relationship Unveiled:

To comprehend the multifaceted connection between population dynamics and resource availability, we must first recognize its depth and intricacy:

Population Size and Growth:

The global population stands at an astounding 7.9 billion individuals, a number that continues to climb. This ever-increasing headcount is a testament to humanity's adaptability and resilience. Yet, it also raises profound questions about our ability to sustain such numbers in the long term.

Resource Utilization:

Our planet offers a finite pool of resources—freshwater, arable land, minerals, and more—that sustains life. These resources are not boundless, and their availability is finite. The challenge lies in managing them effectively to meet the needs of a growing global population.

Distribution Disparities:

The distribution of both people and resources across the globe is far from equitable. Some regions teem with human activity, while others remain sparsely populated. Simultaneously, resource-rich areas coexist with resource-poor regions. Bridging these disparities is a pressing concern.

Resource Depletion:

As the global population burgeons, so does our resource consumption. Some resources, such as fossil fuels and certain minerals, are finite and non-renewable. Overexploitation and depletion of these resources pose significant challenges.

Resource Scarcity:

Water scarcity, soil degradation, and food shortages are already a reality for many. Balancing resource availability with the demands of a growing population is a delicate act, one that requires innovation and sustainable practices.

The Nexus of Challenges and Opportunities:

Our analysis of population and resource interactions underscores the need for proactive measures:

1. **Sustainable Resource Management:** Implementing sustainable practices in agriculture, energy production, and resource extraction is imperative. This includes reducing

waste, recycling, and adopting circular economy principles.

2. **Innovation and Technology:** Harnessing innovation, such as advanced farming techniques and clean energy solutions, can help meet the needs of a growing population while minimizing environmental impacts.

3. **Equitable Distribution:** Addressing disparities in resource distribution and access is essential. Initiatives to promote fairness in resource allocation and wealth distribution are vital.

4. **Population Stabilization:** Encouraging family planning and education can help stabilize population growth. Empowering women with choices regarding family size is a key component of this effort.

5. **Climate Action:** Climate change exacerbates resource challenges. Mitigating climate change through emissions reduction and climate-resilient infrastructure is integral to resource sustainability.

Charting the Course Ahead:

Our exploration of population and resource dynamics unveils both the intricacies of this relationship and the imperative for action. As we navigate this complex terrain, we will continue to dissect these interactions, unveiling insights, strategies, and examples of positive change that inspire hope for a balanced and sustainable future.

As we navigate this section, we'll aim to answer critical questions about the state of our world's resources. Are we on a path towards sustainability, or are we depleting resources at an unsustainable rate? What actions can be taken to ensure a brighter and more sustainable future?

Section 2: The Future of Jobs and Living

Evolving Workforce Dynamics:

Automation and Artificial Intelligence (AI): Automation is transforming industries by streamlining routine tasks, while AI is revolutionizing decision-making processes. These technologies affect various sectors, including manufacturing, data entry, and customer service. Jobs are evolving or becoming automated, prompting workers to acquire new skills in AI-related fields such as machine learning, data science, and AI ethics.

Gig Economy and Remote Work: The gig economy offers flexibility but introduces job insecurity. Remote work is on the rise, impacting job stability and work-life balance. It's important to understand the benefits and challenges of the gig economy and to prioritize financial planning and job security. Maintaining work-life balance in remote work settings is crucial, and strategies exist for achieving it.

Skills and Lifelong Learning: In today's rapidly changing job market, continuous skill development is essential. This section explores diverse avenues for acquiring new skills, including online education platforms, vocational training, and professional development opportunities. Adaptability and the ability to acquire new skills are critical in an ever-evolving technological landscape.

Challenges in Daily Life:

Urbanization and Infrastructure: Urbanization trends affect transportation, housing, and overall quality of life. While urban areas offer opportunities, they can also bring congestion and housing affordability challenges. Efficient urban planning and sustainable infrastructure development are key to creating livable and environmentally friendly cities.

Environmental Sustainability: Daily life choices significantly impact the environment. This section discusses sustainable practices such as energy conservation, waste reduction, responsible consumption, and sustainable transportation. It explores strategies for individuals to reduce their carbon footprint and contribute to environmental sustainability.

Mental Health and Well-being: Modern life's pace can impact mental health. This section explores strategies for maintaining mental health, including stress management techniques, mindfulness practices, and accessing professional support when needed. It emphasizes work-life balance and inclusive workplace practices that support employee well-being.

Opportunities on the Horizon:

Entrepreneurship and Innovation: Entrepreneurship and innovation drive economic growth. This section explores innovative startups, small businesses, and their role in shaping the job market. It delves into entrepreneurship's potential to address societal challenges and create new markets. Real-world examples illustrate the impact of innovation on job opportunities and economic prosperity.

Community and Social Impact: Community engagement and social impact initiatives bring about positive change. This section explores how individuals and organizations address critical issues like poverty alleviation and environmental conservation. It emphasizes collective action and social entrepreneurship as means to address societal challenges and create meaningful change.

Adaptive Lifestyles: Flexibility and adaptability are crucial. This section explores adaptive lifestyles, including remote work, freelancing, and portfolio careers. It provides strategies for building diverse skill sets and remaining resilient in dynamic environments.

Population Growth and Urbanization

The relentless growth of the global population is an undeniable reality, and its effects on urbanization are profound. As more people migrate to urban centers, cities will continue to expand both horizontally and vertically. Megacities, those with populations exceeding ten million, will become increasingly common. This rapid urbanization presents both challenges and opportunities.

Challenges of Urbanization

1. **Infrastructure Strain:** Accommodating a growing urban population demands significant investments in infrastructure. The strain on transportation systems, housing, sanitation, and utilities can lead to congestion and service deficiencies if not adequately addressed.

2. **Resource Consumption:** Urban areas consume vast amounts of resources, from energy to water and land. Managing these resources sustainably will be crucial for minimizing environmental impact.

3. **Social Inequality:** Rapid urbanization can exacerbate social inequalities. Access to quality

education, healthcare, and job opportunities can be unevenly distributed, leading to disparities in living standards.

Opportunities of Urbanization

1. **Innovation Hubs:** Cities are hubs of innovation, attracting talent and fostering creativity. They offer opportunities for entrepreneurship, research, and development, driving economic growth.

2. **Sustainability Initiatives:** Urban areas can lead the way in sustainability efforts. Investments in green infrastructure, public transportation, and renewable energy can make cities more environmentally friendly.

3. **Cultural Diversity:** Cities are melting pots of culture and diversity. Interactions between people from different backgrounds can lead to cultural enrichment and a broader perspective on global issues.

Changing Nature of Work

Advancements in technology, particularly in automation and artificial intelligence, are poised to reshape the job landscape. While these changes come with challenges, they also offer new opportunities for individuals and society as a whole.

Challenges in the Changing Work Environment

1. **Job Displacement:** Automation may lead to job displacement in certain industries. Individuals in routine, manual, or repetitive roles may find their employment prospects diminished.

2. **Skill Gap:** There will be a growing demand for skills related to technology, data analysis, and problem-solving. Bridging the skill gap will be essential to ensure that the workforce remains competitive.

3. **Job Insecurity:** The gig economy and flexible work arrangements may provide job opportunities but also bring job insecurity without traditional job security benefits.

Opportunities in the Changing Work Environment

1. **New Job Roles:** As technology advances, new job roles will emerge. These may include positions related to robotics maintenance, data analysis, cybersecurity, and virtual reality development.

2. **Remote Work:** Remote work options will continue to expand, providing flexibility for employees and reducing the need for physical commuting.

3. **Entrepreneurship:** The digital age has lowered barriers to entry for entrepreneurs. More people

can start their businesses, fostering innovation and economic growth.

Sustainable Living and Environmental Concerns

The imperative for sustainable living has never been clearer. The consequences of unsustainable practices, such as resource depletion, pollution, and climate change, are evident. Adapting to a sustainable lifestyle is not just a choice; it's a necessity.

Sustainable Practices for Individuals

1. **Reducing Consumption:** Sustainable living begins with reducing personal consumption. This includes minimizing waste, conserving water and energy, and making eco-conscious purchasing decisions.

2. **Renewable Energy Adoption:** Transitioning to renewable energy sources like solar and wind power reduces reliance on fossil fuels and decreases greenhouse gas emissions.

3. **Eco-Friendly Transportation:** Using public transport, carpooling, biking, or walking can reduce carbon emissions from personal vehicles.

Sustainable Practices for Communities

1. **Urban Planning:** Sustainable urban planning involves designing cities with green spaces, efficient public transportation, and energy-efficient buildings.

2. **Waste Management:** Implementing effective waste management systems, including recycling and composting, helps reduce the environmental impact of urban areas.

3. **Green Initiatives:** Communities can invest in green initiatives such as community gardens, renewable energy projects, and urban forests to enhance sustainability.

Quality of Life and Well-Being

While economic prosperity is essential, it must be accompanied by improvements in quality of life and overall well-being. Ensuring access to essential services and addressing social disparities are central to creating a more equitable future.

Healthcare Access and Universal Coverage

1. **Universal Healthcare:** The establishment of universal healthcare systems can ensure that everyone has access to necessary medical services without financial barriers.

2. **Preventive Care:** Emphasizing preventive care can reduce the burden on healthcare systems and improve overall population health.

Education Opportunities for All

1. **Equal Access to Education:** Ensuring that quality education is accessible to all, regardless of socio-economic background, promotes equality of opportunity.

2. **Vocational Training:** Providing vocational training and skills development programs can prepare individuals for the evolving job market.

Social Safety Nets and Support Systems

1. **Income Support:** Implementing income support programs can protect vulnerable populations during economic downturns or times of crisis.

2. **Mental Health Services:** Recognizing the importance of mental health, communities can invest in accessible mental health services and reduce stigma.

As we delve into the future of jobs and living, it's clear that while challenges exist, proactive measures and innovative strategies can pave the way for a brighter, more sustainable, and equitable future.

Chapter 4: The State of Our Environment in the Future

Section 1: Future Natural Landscapes

The potential state of our natural landscapes, including lakes, rivers, forests, seas, and oceans, is a crucial aspect of understanding the trajectory of our environment in the coming years. As climate change and human activities continue to impact these ecosystems, envisioning their future can help guide our conservation efforts.

Lakes and Rivers

1. **Impact of Climate Change:** Rising temperatures and altered precipitation patterns may lead to changes in lake and river ecosystems. Increased evaporation and reduced water flow could threaten the availability of freshwater resources.

2. **Biodiversity Conservation:** Efforts to protect the biodiversity of these freshwater systems will be crucial. Conservation initiatives and habitat restoration can help safeguard the health of lakes and rivers.

Forests

1. **Climate-Driven Shifts:** Climate change may result in shifts in the geographic distribution of forests. Some regions may experience forest loss due to

increased wildfires, pests, and droughts, while others could see forest expansion.

2. **Biodiversity Conservation:** Protecting the biodiversity within forests is essential. Sustainable logging practices, reforestation efforts, and the preservation of old-growth forests can contribute to forest health.

Seas and Oceans

1. **Ocean Acidification:** Oceans are becoming more acidic due to the absorption of excess carbon dioxide from the atmosphere. This can harm marine life, particularly creatures with calcium carbonate shells, such as corals and mollusks.

2. **Rising Sea Levels:** Sea levels are expected to continue rising due to the melting of polar ice caps and glaciers. This poses a significant threat to coastal communities and ecosystems.

3. **Overfishing and Marine Conservation:** Overfishing remains a concern. Sustainable fisheries management and the establishment of marine protected areas are critical for preserving ocean biodiversity.

4. **Plastic Pollution:** Addressing plastic pollution in the oceans is paramount. Initiatives to reduce single-use plastics and clean up existing plastic waste are essential for the health of marine ecosystems.

5. **Coral Reefs:** Coral reefs face numerous threats, including warming waters and ocean acidification. Conservation efforts, coral restoration, and climate action are vital for their survival.

Understanding the potential future state of these natural landscapes is essential for developing strategies to protect and conserve them. By addressing climate change, implementing sustainable practices, and preserving biodiversity, we can strive for a more harmonious coexistence with the environment in the years to come.

Section 2: Climate and Weather: The Future Outlook

Understanding the future of our climate and weather patterns is of paramount importance as we navigate the challenges of a changing world. Climate change, driven by human activities, is poised to have profound effects on the quality of weather in the years ahead.

Changing Weather Patterns

1. **Temperature Extremes:** The future is likely to witness more frequent and intense temperature extremes. Heatwaves will become more common, with soaring temperatures impacting health, agriculture, and energy demand.

2. **Precipitation Variability:** Changes in precipitation patterns will lead to increased droughts in some regions and heavier rainfall and flooding in others. These shifts will have significant implications for water resources and agriculture.

3. **Extreme Weather Events:** The frequency and severity of extreme weather events, such as hurricanes, cyclones, and wildfires, are expected to rise. Communities will need to adapt to these events and bolster disaster preparedness.

Climate Adaptation and Mitigation

1. **Climate Resilience:** Building climate-resilient infrastructure and communities will be imperative. This includes designing buildings to withstand extreme weather, improving flood defenses, and creating sustainable water management systems.

2. **Renewable Energy:** Transitioning to renewable energy sources is essential for mitigating climate change. Solar, wind, and hydropower will play a crucial role in reducing greenhouse gas emissions.

3. **Carbon Reduction:** Carbon capture and storage technologies, along with reforestation and afforestation efforts, will be vital in curbing the rise of greenhouse gases in the atmosphere.

4. **Global Cooperation:** International cooperation and agreements, such as the Paris Agreement, will be necessary to address climate change on a global scale. Diplomatic efforts must continue to reduce emissions and limit global warming.

Human Impact on Climate

1. **Consumer Behavior:** Reducing our ecological footprint through sustainable consumption practices, such as minimizing waste and choosing eco-friendly products, can contribute to a healthier climate.

2. **Transportation:** Shifting to electric vehicles, promoting public transportation, and reducing air travel emissions are key strategies for combatting climate change.

3. **Education and Advocacy:** Raising awareness about climate change and advocating for policy changes is essential. Public pressure can drive governments and industries to take meaningful action.

The quality of future weather is intricately linked to our actions today. By addressing the root causes of climate change and implementing adaptation and mitigation strategies, we can work towards a future where weather patterns are more stable and conducive to human well-being.

Chapter 5: Food and Water Sustainability

Future Food and Water Availability: Ensuring Sustainability

Ensuring a sustainable and secure food and water supply is one of the most pressing challenges of our time. As the global population continues to grow and environmental pressures mount, a comprehensive analysis of future food and water availability is essential.

Food Sustainability in the Future

1. **Population Growth and Food Demand:** With the world's population projected to reach over 9 billion by mid-century, the demand for food will increase significantly. Ensuring a consistent and nutritious food supply for all will be paramount.

2. **Agricultural Innovation:** Innovations in agriculture, such as precision farming, vertical farming, and aquaponics, will play a crucial role in meeting future food demands while minimizing environmental impact.

3. **Sustainable Practices:** Embracing sustainable agricultural practices, including organic farming and reduced chemical use, can mitigate the

negative environmental effects of food production.

4. **Food Distribution and Access:** Addressing issues of food distribution and access will be vital. Reducing food waste, improving logistics, and implementing fair distribution systems are necessary steps.

Water Sustainability in the Future

1. **Water Scarcity:** Water scarcity is a growing concern. Climate change, pollution, and over-extraction of groundwater pose threats to the availability of clean and freshwater sources.

2. **Efficient Water Use:** Promoting water-efficient technologies in agriculture, industry, and households can help preserve this precious resource.

3. **Water Management:** Effective water management, including watershed protection and the restoration of aquatic ecosystems, is essential for maintaining water quality and quantity.

4. **Desalination and Recycling:** Exploring innovative solutions like desalination and wastewater recycling can provide additional sources of freshwater.

Climate Change Impacts

1. **Climate-Induced Challenges:** Climate change will exacerbate both food and water challenges. More frequent and severe droughts, floods, and storms will disrupt agriculture and water availability.

2. **Adaptive Strategies:** Developing adaptive strategies, such as drought-resistant crop varieties and resilient water infrastructure, is critical to address the impacts of climate change.

Global Cooperation and Policy

1. **International Collaboration:** Addressing food and water challenges requires international cooperation. Agreements and initiatives to manage transboundary water resources and ensure food security will be essential.

2. **Sustainable Development Goals:** Aligning efforts with the United Nations Sustainable Development Goals (SDGs), particularly Goal 2 (Zero Hunger) and Goal 6 (Clean Water and Sanitation), will guide global action.

Community and Individual Actions

1. **Reducing Food Waste:** At the individual level, reducing food waste by mindful consumption and

responsible disposal can contribute to food sustainability.

2. **Water Conservation:** Implementing water-saving practices at home and in communities can help conserve water resources.

Analyzing future food and water availability is not just a matter of ensuring survival; it's about guaranteeing a high quality of life for all while safeguarding the planet's ecosystems. Through responsible practices, innovation, and global collaboration, we can work towards a future where food and water are abundant, sustainable, and accessible to everyone.

Chapter 6: Future Population Trends
Section 1: Population Projections: Navigating the Future

Predict population figures for 2050, 2075, and 3000 years from now.

Predicting future population trends is a complex but essential task. Understanding how the world's population may evolve in the coming decades and millennia informs a wide range of social, economic, and environmental decisions.

Population Trends in the Near Future (2050)

1. **Continued Growth:** By 2050, the global population is projected to reach approximately 9.7 billion people. This growth will be driven by high birth rates in some regions and longer life expectancies worldwide.

2. **Urbanization:** Urban areas will continue to attract populations, leading to the expansion of mega-cities and the development of new urban centers. Urbanization will bring both opportunities and challenges, including increased demand for infrastructure and resources.

3. **Aging Population:** As life expectancies increase, the world will experience an aging population. This demographic shift will have significant

implications for healthcare, social services, and pension systems.

4. **Regional Variations:** Population growth rates will vary by region. Some countries will experience rapid growth, while others will face demographic stagnation or decline. These variations will influence global geopolitics and economic dynamics.

Population Trends in the Mid-Future (2075)

1. **Stabilization:** By 2075, the global population is expected to stabilize, with estimates ranging from 9.7 to 10.2 billion people. This stabilization will result from declining birth rates in many regions.

2. **Urban Dominance:** Urbanization will continue to be a dominant trend. Cities will house the majority of the world's population, leading to challenges related to infrastructure, housing, and resource management.

3. **Environmental Pressures:** As the population stabilizes, the focus will shift to environmental sustainability. Balancing the needs of a large population with the preservation of natural ecosystems will be a central challenge.

4. **Technological Advancements:** Advancements in technology, including automation and artificial intelligence, will reshape the job market and labor

force, impacting employment trends and economic structures.

Population Trends in the Distant Future (3000)

1. **Long-Term Projections:** Predicting the world's population 3000 years from now is highly speculative. However, it raises essential questions about the sustainability of human civilization and our impact on the planet.

2. **Sustainability Challenges:** Addressing long-term population trends requires a focus on sustainability. This includes sustainable resource management, environmental conservation, and responsible governance.

3. **Interstellar Exploration:** Looking even further ahead, humanity may explore other planets and celestial bodies. This could lead to the colonization of other worlds, potentially alleviating some of the pressures on Earth.

4. **Ethical Considerations:** Long-term population projections also raise ethical questions about the responsibilities of current and future generations in preserving the planet and ensuring the well-being of all life.

Adaptive Strategies and Global Collaboration

1. **Resource Management:** To navigate future population trends successfully, sustainable

resource management will be crucial. This includes responsible use of land, water, energy, and food resources.

2. **Education and Healthcare:** Investing in education and healthcare systems is vital for empowering individuals to make informed family planning decisions and ensuring the well-being of all.

3. **International Cooperation:** Global collaboration is essential to address regional disparities in population growth and ensure that sustainable development goals are achieved.

Predicting future population trends is a complex undertaking that involves numerous variables and uncertainties. However, it is a critical endeavor for policymakers, researchers, and society as a whole to plan for a future that balances the needs and aspirations of a growing global population with the preservation of our planet and its resources.

Section 2: Top 10 Largest Nations

1. **China:** With a population of over 1.4 billion people, China remains the most populous country in the world. Its vast population is distributed across diverse regions and cities.

2. **India:** India closely follows China with a population of approximately 1.3 billion. India's population is characterized by its youthfulness and significant cultural diversity.

3. **United States:** The United States is the third-largest nation by population, with over 330 million people. It's known for its immigrant-rich demographics and urban centers.

4. **Indonesia:** Indonesia boasts a population of more than 270 million, making it the fourth-largest nation globally. It's known for its stunning archipelago and rich cultural heritage.

5. **Pakistan:** With a population of around 225 million, Pakistan ranks fifth in terms of population. It's a country with a diverse landscape and a mix of urban and rural populations.

6. **Brazil:** Brazil has over 212 million people, securing its place as the sixth-largest nation by population. It's known for its Amazon rainforest and vibrant cities.

7. **Nigeria:** Nigeria, in West Africa, is the seventh-largest nation, with approximately 206 million inhabitants. It's a country with a youthful population and a growing economy.

8. **Bangladesh:** Bangladesh, with a population of over 165 million, is the eighth-largest nation globally.

It's renowned for its densely populated urban areas and vibrant culture.

9. **Russia:** Russia is the largest nation geographically but ranks ninth in population, with around 145 million people. It spans across vast Eurasian territories.

10. **Mexico:** Mexico rounds out the top ten with a population of approximately 128 million. It's known for its rich history, cuisine, and urban centers.

These ten nations represent a significant portion of the world's population and play critical roles in global politics, economics, and culture. Understanding their demographics is essential for grasping the complexities of the global population landscape.

Population Projections for 2050, 2075, and 3000:

Estimating population figures for the future involves various factors, including birth rates, death rates, migration, and other demographic dynamics. Birth rates can change over time due to social, economic, and cultural factors. However, I can provide a rough projection based on current trends and assumptions, but please note that these are speculative and subject to change. Additionally, predicting population figures for 3000 years into the future is highly uncertain. Here's a rough estimate for the specified years:

1. **China:**

   - 2050: Around 1.4 billion
   - 2075: Around 1.3 billion
   - 3000: Highly uncertain, but potentially lower due to a declining birth rate.

2. **India:**

   - 2050: Around 1.7 billion (projected to surpass China)
   - 2075: Around 1.8 billion
   - 3000: Highly uncertain, but potentially continuing to grow due to a relatively high birth rate.

3. **United States:**

   - 2050: Around 400 million
   - 2075: Around 430 million
   - 3000: Highly uncertain, but potentially higher with continued immigration and a relatively stable birth rate.

4. **Indonesia:**

   - 2050: Around 300 million
   - 2075: Around 320 million
   - 3000: Highly uncertain, but potentially continuing to grow due to a moderate birth rate.

5. **Pakistan:**

- 2050: Around 340 million

- 2075: Around 380 million

- 3000: Highly uncertain, but potentially continuing to grow due to a relatively high birth rate.

6. **Brazil:**

- 2050: Around 240 million

- 2075: Around 250 million

- 3000: Highly uncertain, but potentially stabilizing or declining due to a decreasing birth rate.

7. **Nigeria:**

- 2050: Around 450 million

- 2075: Around 500 million

- 3000: Highly uncertain, but potentially continuing to grow due to a high birth rate.

8. **Bangladesh:**

- 2050: Around 210 million

- 2075: Around 220 million

- 3000: Highly uncertain, but potentially continuing to grow due to a moderate birth rate.

9. **Russia:**

- 2050: Around 140 million

- 2075: Around 135 million

- 3000: Highly uncertain, but potentially declining due to a low birth rate and other factors.

10. **Mexico:**

- 2050: Around 150 million

- 2075: Around 160 million

- 3000: Highly uncertain, but potentially stabilizing or declining due to a decreasing birth rate.

These projections are speculative, and actual population figures may differ significantly depending on future developments in each country's demographics, healthcare, and socioeconomic conditions.

Chapter 7: Nations at Risk

Nations Facing Extinction

Predicting which nations may face population decline or extinction in the distant future, such as 2050, 2075, or 3000, involves numerous complex factors and uncertainties. While it's challenging to make precise predictions, we can speculate based on current demographic trends, environmental conditions, and potential scenarios. Please keep in mind that these are speculative scenarios and should be taken as such.

2050:

- **Low-Lying Island Nations:** Small, low-lying island nations in the Pacific Ocean, such as Tuvalu, Kiribati, and the Marshall Islands, may face significant challenges due to rising sea levels and climate change. These nations may experience displacement of their populations, making them vulnerable to extinction.

2075:

- **Small European Nations:** Some small European nations with declining birth rates and aging populations, like Monaco, Andorra, and San Marino, may continue to experience population decline. While not facing immediate extinction, their populations could become critically small.

3000:

- **Antarctica:** Antarctica is a continent with no native human population. However, due to climate change, if conditions worsen significantly, it could become even more inhospitable, making any human presence extremely challenging. This isn't a nation but a region.

It's important to note that these scenarios are highly speculative, and various factors, including technological advancements, policy changes, and global events, can alter the course of population trends. Additionally, efforts to mitigate climate change and address demographic challenges may impact these projections.

The prospect of entire nations facing extinction is a grave concern, and global cooperation and proactive measures are essential to prevent or mitigate such scenarios.

Risk at Central Asian Countries

The scenario you describe, where small countries in Central Asia or neighboring regions experience significant immigration from countries like China and India, can have complex demographic, social, and economic implications. Here are some factors to consider:

1. Demographic Impact:

- Small countries with populations of 6 million or less are more vulnerable to demographic shifts. Significant immigration from larger countries can lead to a rapid increase in population size.

- Intermarriage between immigrants and locals can further complicate demographic changes, potentially altering the ethnic and cultural composition of these nations.

2. Economic Impact:

- Immigration, if well-managed, can contribute to economic growth by bringing in new skills, labor, and investments.

- The financial incentives offered by countries like China for business and marriage could stimulate economic activity in these smaller nations.

3. Cultural and Social Impact:

- Increased cultural diversity resulting from immigration can enrich a nation's cultural fabric but may also pose challenges related to integration and identity.

- Changes in social norms, languages, and traditions may occur due to intermarriage and cultural exchange.

4. Governance and Sustainability:

- Small nations may face governance challenges in managing rapid population growth and ensuring equitable distribution of resources and services.

- Sustainability concerns may arise if immigration leads to increased pressure on local resources and ecosystems.

5. Diplomatic Relations:

- Governments of small nations will need to navigate diplomatic relations with larger neighbors to ensure that immigration is managed effectively and does not lead to conflicts or social tensions.

Overall, the impact of immigration on small countries depends on various factors, including government policies, the rate of immigration, the capacity to integrate newcomers, and the willingness of both immigrants and locals to adapt to changing circumstances.

Governments of these small countries should develop clear immigration policies and strategies that balance economic opportunities with the preservation of their unique cultural identities and environmental sustainability. Collaborative efforts with larger neighbors can help manage immigration in ways that benefit both parties while safeguarding the interests of local populations.

Turkey's Position

Issues of immigration, demographics, cultural change, and societal dynamics

1. **Afghan Immigration to Turkey**: Many Afghan men are escaping to Turkey, presumably due to various factors, such as conflict, economic hardship, or political instability in Afghanistan. Immigration is a global phenomenon, and countries like Turkey have been destinations for people seeking better lives or safety.

2. **Immigrant Population in Turkey**: Turkey has a substantial immigrant population, with a significant number coming from Syria and Afghanistan. This has implications for social and economic dynamics within the country, including access to resources, job opportunities, and public services.

3. **Demographics and Family Size**: Many immigrants marry early and have large families, with at least

five children and sometimes more than one wife. This can indeed impact the demographic composition of the country. High birth rates can lead to population growth and influence the distribution of resources.

4. **Cultural and Racial Landscape**: The cultural and racial landscape of a nation is constantly evolving, influenced by immigration, intermarriage, and the adaptation of new cultural elements. In the case of Turkey, a diverse immigrant population can contribute to cultural diversity and enrich the societal tapestry. However, it can also pose challenges related to integration and social cohesion.

5. **Future Implications**: The long-term implications of these demographic and cultural changes are complex. They depend on various factors, including government policies, social integration efforts, and economic conditions. It's possible that Turkey's cultural and racial landscape will become more diverse over time, but the specifics will depend on numerous factors.

6. **Integration and Challenges**: Successful integration of immigrants into Turkish society is crucial for addressing potential challenges. Integration efforts typically involve providing access to education, healthcare, employment opportunities, and pathways to citizenship. It also

involves promoting social cohesion and understanding among different communities.

In summary, the situation described highlights the ongoing dynamics of immigration and its impact on a host country's demographic and cultural landscape. Turkey, like many other nations, will need to navigate these changes thoughtfully to ensure the well-being and integration of its immigrant populations while addressing any potential challenges that may arise.

However, we can make some general observations based on current trends and historical context:

1. **2050 and 2075**:

   - By 2050 and 2075, Turkey's demographic landscape will likely continue to be shaped by immigration, as well as natural population growth.

   - The specific immigrant populations may evolve, but given Turkey's geographic location between Europe and Asia and its historical role as a crossroads, it's likely to remain a destination for immigrants from various regions.

   - Government policies, economic conditions, and global events will play a significant role in determining the scale and composition of immigration during these periods.

2. **3000 Years**:

- Predicting the state of Turkey or any nation 3000 years into the future is highly speculative and largely beyond the scope of current forecasting methodologies.

- Over such an extended time frame, countless geopolitical, environmental, and technological changes could occur, making it impossible to provide a detailed outlook.

- Long-term predictions often involve factors like climate change, technological advancements, and geopolitical shifts, which are difficult to anticipate with accuracy.

It's important to note that demographic changes are just one aspect of a nation's future. Turkey's trajectory will depend on a wide range of factors, including political developments, economic stability, environmental challenges, and global events. Government policies and societal decisions will also play a crucial role in shaping the country's future.

In conclusion, while we can make educated guesses about Turkey's near-term demographic trends, predicting its situation 3000 years from now is purely speculative, and it's more productive to focus on addressing current challenges and making informed decisions in the present.

Risk for Turkey

Demographic projections for specific ethnic or cultural groups over such long time frames (2050 years, 2075, and 3000 years) are highly speculative and depend on numerous factors, including birth rates, immigration patterns, government policies, and social changes. However, here some general insights:

1. **Kurdish Population**:

   - The Kurdish population in Turkey has historically had a higher birth rate compared to some other groups. If this trend continues, the Kurdish population could continue to grow as a percentage of the overall population.

2. **Arab and Afghan Immigrants**:

   - The growth of the Arab and Afghan immigrant populations will depend on several factors, including immigration rates, birth rates among these groups, and potential changes in immigration policies.

3. **Turkic Population**:

- Turkic people in Turkey may have a lower birth rate compared to some other groups. However, this can change over time due to various factors, including cultural shifts and government policies.

4. **Overall Population Growth**:

- Turkey's overall population growth will be influenced by the combined effects of birth rates, mortality rates, and immigration. It's challenging to make precise projections without detailed data and complex modeling.

5. **Government Policies and Social Changes**:

- Government policies and societal changes can have a significant impact on demographic trends. Policies that promote or discourage certain behaviors, such as family planning, can influence birth rates.

6. **Environmental and Economic Factors**:

- Long-term demographic projections are also influenced by environmental factors, such as access to healthcare and resources, as well as economic conditions that affect family planning decisions.

For projections specific to 2050 years, 2075, and 3000 years into the future, it's important to emphasize that making precise predictions is impossible. Demographic changes are highly dynamic and subject to a wide range of influences. Government policies, societal attitudes, and global events can all shape the future demographic landscape.

Chapter 8: Biodiversity and Extinction

Endangered Species

1. Habitat Destruction

Deforestation, the large-scale removal of forests for various purposes, stands as one of the most pressing environmental challenges of our time. This widespread practice encompasses activities like logging for timber, clearing land for agriculture, and urban expansion. The consequences of deforestation are far-reaching:

The Impact on Biodiversity: Forests are incredibly biodiverse ecosystems, housing millions of plant and animal species, many of which are yet to be discovered. Deforestation disrupts these intricate webs of life, driving countless species to the brink of extinction.

Climate Change: Forests serve as carbon sinks, absorbing carbon dioxide from the atmosphere and helping regulate the Earth's climate. When trees are cut down or burned, this stored carbon is released, contributing to greenhouse gas emissions and global warming.

Erosion and Soil Degradation: The removal of trees leaves soil exposed to erosion by wind and water. This leads to loss of fertile topsoil, reducing agricultural productivity and affecting local communities that depend on the land for sustenance.

Loss of Ecosystem Services: Forests provide essential ecosystem services like clean water, pollination of crops, and protection against natural disasters. Deforestation jeopardizes these services, impacting human well-being and livelihoods.

Urbanization: The rapid growth of cities and urban areas is a defining feature of the modern world. Urbanization brings economic opportunities and improved living standards for many, but it also comes with significant environmental challenges:

Habitat Conversion: As cities expand, they encroach on natural habitats, leading to the destruction of forests, wetlands, and other ecosystems. This displacement affects local wildlife and disrupts ecological balance.

Urban Heat Islands: The concentration of buildings, roads, and concrete in urban areas creates urban heat islands. These regions experience higher temperatures than surrounding rural areas, impacting energy consumption, human health, and local ecosystems.

Transportation and Pollution: Urbanization is often accompanied by increased traffic and industrial activities, leading to higher levels of air and water pollution. This pollution can harm human health and have detrimental effects on urban ecosystems.

Infrastructure Development: The construction of roads, bridges, and buildings in urban areas alters the landscape and can disrupt natural drainage patterns, leading to flooding and other environmental challenges.

Agriculture: Agriculture is the backbone of food production and a key driver of human civilization. However, modern agricultural practices have raised important environmental concerns:

Monoculture Farming: Large-scale monoculture farming focuses on single crop varieties, which can lead to soil degradation, reduced biodiversity, and increased susceptibility to pests and diseases.

Chemical Inputs: The use of chemical fertilizers and pesticides in agriculture can harm ecosystems and pose risks to human health. Runoff from agricultural fields can contaminate waterways and aquatic ecosystems.

Land Use Change: The expansion of agricultural land often involves clearing forests or draining wetlands. This can result in habitat loss, increased greenhouse gas emissions, and disruption of natural ecosystems.

Sustainable Agriculture: There is growing recognition of the need for sustainable farming practices that prioritize soil health, biodiversity, and reduced chemical inputs. Sustainable agriculture aims to meet the world's food needs while minimizing its environmental footprint.

These challenges associated with deforestation, urbanization, and agriculture highlight the complex relationship between human activities and the environment. Addressing these issues requires a holistic approach that balances economic development with environmental conservation and sustainability.

2. Climate Change Impact

Climate change poses a significant threat to species across the globe. We'll delve into the impacts of rising temperatures, shifting weather patterns, and sea-level rise on vulnerable ecosystems and species. Understanding these consequences is essential for developing strategies to mitigate climate-related threats and protect biodiversity.

Climate change, driven primarily by human activities such as the burning of fossil fuels and deforestation, has emerged as one of the most critical challenges facing our planet. Its far-reaching impacts extend to various ecosystems and species, with profound consequences:

Rising Temperatures: The global average temperature is on the rise, leading to higher temperatures in many regions. This can disrupt the natural behavior and habitats of numerous species, affecting their reproduction, migration patterns, and survival.

Shifting Weather Patterns: Climate change alters weather patterns, leading to more frequent and severe weather events such as hurricanes, droughts, and floods. These extreme events can have devastating effects on wildlife and their habitats.

Sea-Level Rise: As global temperatures increase, polar ice caps and glaciers are melting, causing sea levels to rise. Coastal habitats and the species that depend on them are particularly vulnerable to this phenomenon, facing habitat loss and increased salinity.

Altered Migration and Breeding: Many species rely on specific temperature and weather cues for migration and breeding. Changes in these cues can disrupt these critical life events, leading to population declines.

Ocean Acidification: Increased carbon dioxide levels in the atmosphere also contribute to ocean acidification. This can harm marine life, especially those with calcium carbonate shells or skeletons, such as corals and shellfish.

Loss of Polar Habitats: The polar regions are particularly sensitive to climate change, with rapidly melting ice affecting species like polar bears and penguins. Loss of sea ice also impacts the availability of food for marine mammals and birds.

Ecosystem Disruption: Climate change can disrupt entire ecosystems by affecting the timing of natural events like flowering and pollination, predator-prey relationships, and the availability of resources. This can have cascading effects on multiple species within an ecosystem.

Understanding these consequences of climate change is essential for developing strategies to mitigate its impacts on vulnerable ecosystems and species. Conservation efforts must prioritize adaptation and resilience-building to help wildlife cope with changing conditions. Additionally, global efforts to reduce greenhouse gas emissions are crucial for slowing down the pace of climate change and protecting biodiversity.

3. Poaching and Illegal Wildlife Trade

The illegal wildlife trade remains a grave concern for many species. We'll delve into the drivers behind poaching and the illegal trade in animals and their parts, including the economic incentives and cultural factors. Our exploration will highlight the critical role of law enforcement, international cooperation, and community engagement in combating this illicit activity.

Poaching and the illegal wildlife trade represent a dire threat to many species around the world. These activities are driven by a complex interplay of factors, including economic incentives, cultural practices, and demand for exotic products. Let's delve into the dynamics of this issue:

Economic Incentives: Poaching often offers economic opportunities to individuals in impoverished regions. The sale of wildlife products, such as ivory, rhino horns, and exotic pets, can fetch high prices on the black market, making it an attractive option for those seeking financial gain.

Cultural Factors: In some cultures, certain wildlife products are highly prized for their perceived medicinal or status-enhancing properties. Traditional beliefs and practices can drive demand for these items, further fueling the illegal trade.

Global Demand: The illegal wildlife trade is not confined to local markets. There is a global demand for exotic pets, luxury goods made from animal parts, and traditional medicines, driving poaching activities in different parts of the world.

Habitat Loss: Poaching is often linked to habitat loss. As natural habitats shrink due to human activities, such as deforestation and urbanization, wildlife is pushed into smaller, more vulnerable areas, making them easier targets for poachers.

Law Enforcement: Effective law enforcement is crucial in combating poaching and the illegal wildlife trade. This includes efforts to apprehend poachers, dismantle trafficking networks, and prosecute those involved in the trade.

International Cooperation: Since the illegal wildlife trade is a global issue, international cooperation is essential. Agreements such as the Convention on International Trade in Endangered Species of Wild Fauna and Flora (CITES) facilitate collaboration among countries to regulate and monitor the trade in endangered species.

Community Engagement: Engaging local communities in conservation efforts is vital. Providing alternative livelihoods, raising awareness about the importance of wildlife, and involving communities in anti-poaching initiatives can reduce the incentives for poaching.

Tackling poaching and the illegal wildlife trade requires a multi-faceted approach that addresses both the supply and demand sides of the issue. This includes strengthening law enforcement, addressing economic disparities, raising awareness, and promoting sustainable alternatives to poaching. Ultimately, combating this illicit activity is essential to protect endangered species and preserve global biodiversity.

4. Pollution and Toxins

Pollution, including chemical pollutants and plastic waste, affects ecosystems and species worldwide. Recognizing the role of pollution in species decline is essential for advocating for cleaner environments and more sustainable practices.

Pollution, whether in the form of chemical pollutants or plastic waste, exerts a significant and far-reaching impact on ecosystems and species across the globe. Let's explore the consequences of pollution on both aquatic and terrestrial environments, as well as its indirect effects on species through food chains:

Chemical Pollutants: Various industrial, agricultural, and household chemicals find their way into the environment, contaminating soil, water, and air. These pollutants can have direct and indirect effects on species. For example, pesticides can harm non-target organisms, including beneficial insects and birds, while runoff from agricultural fields can lead to "dead zones" in aquatic ecosystems.

Plastic Pollution: Plastic waste, especially in the form of microplastics, has become a pervasive issue in oceans and other water bodies. Marine species, such as sea turtles and seabirds, often ingest plastic debris, leading to physical harm and ingestion of toxic chemicals. Additionally, microplastics can enter the food chain, potentially impacting species at various trophic levels.

Aquatic Environments: Aquatic ecosystems are particularly vulnerable to pollution. Chemical pollutants can disrupt the health of freshwater and marine species, affecting their reproductive success and overall survival. For instance, heavy metals like mercury can accumulate in fish, posing risks to both aquatic life and human consumers.

Terrestrial Environments: Pollution can also harm species in terrestrial ecosystems. Air pollution, for example, can damage plant life and alter soil composition, indirectly affecting herbivores and predators that rely on these resources. Additionally, pollutants can lead to the decline of pollinators, which are essential for many plant species' reproduction.

Food Chain Effects: Pollution doesn't only impact species directly; it can also affect entire food chains. Contaminated prey can transfer toxins up the food chain, leading to bioaccumulation in predators. This bioaccumulation can result in reproductive issues, weakened immune systems, and reduced population sizes in apex predators.

Advocating for Cleaner Environments: Recognizing the role of pollution in species decline underscores the urgency of advocating for cleaner environments and more sustainable practices. This includes reducing the use of harmful chemicals, implementing waste management strategies to mitigate plastic pollution, and enforcing regulations to limit industrial emissions.

Scientific Research: Ongoing scientific research plays a critical role in understanding the specific impacts of pollutants on different species and ecosystems. This knowledge informs conservation efforts and policy decisions aimed at reducing pollution's harm to biodiversity.

By delving into the multifaceted issue of pollution and toxins, we gain insight into the challenges faced by species worldwide. Addressing these challenges requires concerted efforts to reduce pollution at its source, mitigate its effects on ecosystems, and protect the health of both wildlife and humans.

5. Invasive Species

Invasive species pose a significant threat to native flora and fauna, as they can outcompete local species, disrupt ecosystems, and lead to population declines and extinctions. Let's explore the challenges posed by invasive species, including their introduction and spread:

Introduction: Invasive species are typically non-native organisms that are introduced to new environments, often unintentionally. They can arrive through various means, including trade, travel, and shipping. These introductions can occur via the transport of goods, ballast water from ships, or even as hitchhikers on vehicles and clothing.

Spread: Once introduced, invasive species can establish populations and spread rapidly. Their ability to outcompete native species is often due to a lack of natural predators or competitors in their new habitat. They can also adapt to local conditions, making them formidable competitors.

Impact on Biodiversity: Invasive species can have a profound impact on biodiversity. They may outcompete native species for resources such as food, water, and shelter. In doing so, they can reduce the abundance and diversity of native species, sometimes leading to their decline or extinction.

Ecosystem Disruption: Invasive species can disrupt entire ecosystems. For example, the introduction of invasive plants can alter soil composition and fire regimes. Invasive animals can prey on or compete with native species, causing cascading effects throughout the food web.

Economic Costs: Invasive species also come with significant economic costs. They can damage crops, impact fisheries, and increase the expenses associated with pest control and eradication efforts. These costs can burden agriculture, forestry, and other industries.

Early Detection and Management: Addressing the challenges posed by invasive species requires early detection and effective management strategies. Early detection programs, such as monitoring at ports and borders, are crucial for identifying and responding to potential invaders before they become established.

Management Strategies: Managing invasive species often involves a combination of strategies, including physical removal, chemical control, and biological control using natural predators or diseases. These strategies must be carefully considered to minimize unintended harm to native species and ecosystems.

International Cooperation: Invasive species are a global issue, and international cooperation is essential to address their spread. Countries work together to develop guidelines, regulations, and strategies for preventing and managing invasive species.

Public Awareness: Raising public awareness about the risks associated with invasive species is vital. Education campaigns can help individuals take steps to prevent the unintentional introduction and spread of invasive species, such as cleaning hiking boots to prevent the spread of plant seeds.

By delving into the challenges posed by invasive species, we gain a deeper understanding of the need for proactive measures to prevent their introduction, detect them early, and effectively manage their populations. Protecting native biodiversity from the impacts of invasive species is a critical component of conservation efforts worldwide.

6. Conservation Strategies

Amid the threats facing endangered species, conservation efforts offer hope. By understanding the successes and challenges of these approaches, we can support and advocate for effective conservation measures.

In the face of numerous threats to endangered species, conservation efforts provide a glimmer of hope. Let's delve into various strategies employed to protect and restore populations, including:

Captive Breeding Programs: Captive breeding involves breeding endangered species in controlled environments, such as zoos or specialized facilities. This strategy helps increase population numbers and genetic diversity. However, it requires careful management to prevent inbreeding and maintain genetic health.

Habitat Restoration: Habitat destruction is a primary driver of species endangerment. Habitat restoration involves repairing and revitalizing ecosystems that have been damaged or degraded. This may include reforesting areas, restoring wetlands, or removing invasive species to recreate suitable habitats for endangered species.

Reintroduction Programs: Reintroduction programs aim to return captive-bred or rehabilitated animals to their natural habitats. Successful reintroductions can help reestablish self-sustaining populations in the wild. However, they must consider factors like habitat suitability, disease risks, and human interactions.

Protected Areas: Establishing protected areas, such as national parks and reserves, can safeguard critical habitats for endangered species. These areas provide safe havens where wildlife can thrive without the pressures of habitat destruction and hunting.

Community-Based Conservation: Involving local communities in conservation efforts is essential. Community-based conservation programs engage residents in the protection of local wildlife and habitats, emphasizing the interconnectedness of human well-being and ecological health.

International Cooperation: Many endangered species have ranges that span multiple countries. International cooperation and agreements, such as the Convention on International Trade in Endangered Species of Wild Fauna and Flora (CITES), facilitate collaborative efforts to protect species and combat illegal wildlife trade.

Education and Awareness: Raising awareness about endangered species and their conservation needs is crucial. Educational programs, public campaigns, and outreach initiatives can inspire individuals and communities to take action and support conservation efforts.

Research and Monitoring: Continuous research and monitoring provide valuable data for conservation decisions. This includes studying the behavior, ecology, and genetics of endangered species, as well as tracking population trends and the effectiveness of conservation measures.

Legislation and Policy: Strong legal frameworks and policies are essential for protecting endangered species. Laws regulating habitat destruction, hunting, and the trade of endangered species help enforce conservation efforts.

Sustainable Practices: Encouraging sustainable practices in agriculture, forestry, and fisheries can mitigate threats to endangered species. Sustainable resource management considers the long-term impact on ecosystems and biodiversity.

Philanthropy and Funding: Conservation organizations, government agencies, and philanthropic individuals and foundations play a crucial role in funding and supporting conservation initiatives.

By delving into these conservation strategies, we gain insights into the multifaceted approach needed to protect and restore endangered species. These efforts require collaboration, innovation, and dedication to ensure the survival and recovery of species on the brink of extinction.

7. Ethical Considerations

The conservation of endangered species is not merely a scientific or practical endeavor; it also delves into complex ethical and moral dimensions.

Let's explore the various ethical considerations that surround species preservation:

Intrinsic Value: One of the central ethical debates in conservation revolves around the intrinsic value of species. This perspective argues that each species has inherent worth and a right to exist, regardless of its utility to humans. It challenges anthropocentric viewpoints that prioritize human interests above all else.

Anthropocentrism: Anthropocentrism places human interests and well-being at the center of ethical considerations. It questions whether our ethical responsibilities extend to non-human species and ecosystems and whether we should prioritize their preservation.

Biodiversity's Importance: Maintaining biodiversity is not just a matter of ethics; it is also crucial for the health and resilience of ecosystems. Diverse ecosystems provide essential services, such as clean air and water, pollination, and climate regulation, which directly benefit humans.

De-extinction Technologies: Advances in biotechnology raise ethical questions about the de-extinction of extinct species. Delving into these discussions involves examining the potential benefits, risks, and ethical implications of reviving species through genetic engineering or cloning.

Intergenerational Ethics: Species preservation has intergenerational implications. Ethical considerations encompass our responsibility to future generations, as our actions today can impact the biodiversity they inherit.

The Moral Imperative: Many argue that protecting endangered species is a moral imperative. This perspective highlights our ethical duty to act as stewards of the planet, ensuring the survival of species for future generations.

Complex Decision-Making: Conservation decisions often involve complex trade-offs and ethical dilemmas. For example, prioritizing the preservation of one species may require resources that could benefit others. These decisions must balance immediate needs with long-term sustainability.

Community Involvement: Ethical conservation practices consider the rights and interests of local communities. Engaging and respecting the perspectives of indigenous and local communities is integral to ethical conservation efforts.

Environmental Justice: Environmental justice concerns the equitable distribution of environmental benefits and burdens. Ethical considerations include addressing the disproportionate impacts of species extinction on vulnerable and marginalized communities.

Legal and Policy Frameworks: Ethical principles often find expression in legal and policy frameworks. Legislation and international agreements aim to reflect ethical values by protecting endangered species and their habitats.

Education and Awareness: Ethical considerations extend to the broader public. Raising awareness about the ethical dimensions of conservation can engage individuals and communities in meaningful actions to protect endangered species.

By delving into these ethical considerations, we gain a deeper understanding of the complex and interconnected ethical, ecological, and societal issues surrounding the conservation of endangered species. These ethical perspectives play a crucial role in shaping our approach to preserving biodiversity and our relationship with the natural world.

Through this comprehensive exploration, we aim to shed light on the critical importance of preserving the incredible diversity of life on Earth. Endangered species are not just statistics; they are unique, irreplaceable facets of our planet's natural heritage. By understanding the challenges they face and the efforts being made to save them, we can contribute to a more sustainable and harmonious coexistence with the natural world.

Chapter 9: Population Reduction Strategies

Examine potential strategies for population reduction.

In this chapter and in sections, we will delve into various potential strategies for population reduction. It is important to note that discussions about population reduction are highly sensitive and ethically complex. The aim of this exploration is to provide an overview of different strategies that have been proposed or implemented and to consider their ethical, social, and practical implications.

1. Family Planning and Reproductive Health Education:

Access to family planning resources and comprehensive reproductive health education is considered one of the most ethical and effective strategies for population management. It empowers individuals and couples to make informed decisions about family size and spacing, ultimately leading to smaller family sizes.

Empowering Informed Choices: Reproductive health education equips individuals with the knowledge and tools necessary to make informed choices about their reproductive lives. It covers topics such as contraception methods, family planning, and the importance of spacing pregnancies. This education extends beyond simply informing individuals about contraceptive options; it encourages open and honest conversations about family planning within relationships and communities.

Contraception Access: Ensuring access to a variety of contraception methods, including barrier methods, hormonal contraceptives, and long-acting reversible contraceptives (LARCs), is a crucial component of family planning. Accessible contraception options allow individuals and couples to make choices that align with their family planning goals, contributing to lower fertility rates. Comprehensive healthcare systems should include family planning services, making contraception readily available to those who seek it.

Maternal and Child Health: Family planning goes beyond birth control; it encompasses maternal and child health. By providing information on prenatal and postnatal care, as well as child health and nutrition, reproductive health education contributes to healthier pregnancies and reduces child mortality. This, in turn, can influence family size decisions as healthier children often lead to reduced desire for larger families.

Addressing Stigma and Myths: In many societies, there are stigmas and misconceptions associated with contraception and reproductive health. Effective education programs tackle these issues head-on by providing accurate information and addressing common myths. Dispelling misconceptions and reducing stigma can encourage more widespread use of contraception. Education helps individuals understand the safety and benefits of contraception, ultimately leading to greater acceptance and utilization.

Inclusivity and Cultural Sensitivity: Successful reproductive health education programs recognize the diversity of beliefs, values, and practices related to family planning. They tailor their approach to be inclusive and culturally sensitive, ensuring that information and services are accessible to a wide range of communities. Cultural sensitivity ensures that education respects the traditions and values of various cultural and religious groups while still delivering essential information.

Youth Education: Young people benefit significantly from reproductive health education. Comprehensive sex education programs help them make responsible choices about their sexual and reproductive health, reducing the likelihood of early and unplanned pregnancies. By delaying childbearing until later in life, young people often choose to have fewer children. Education also promotes healthier lifestyles, contributing to lower fertility rates among younger populations.

Community Outreach: Community-based programs play a vital role in ensuring that reproductive health education reaches underserved populations. These programs may include mobile clinics, community health workers, and partnerships with local organizations. These initiatives improve access to contraception and education, especially in remote or marginalized areas where healthcare services may be limited.

Ethical Considerations: Throughout our exploration of family planning and reproductive health education, we consider ethical dimensions, including issues related to informed consent, privacy, and reproductive autonomy. These ethical considerations guide the design and implementation of effective programs. Respect for individuals' choices and their right to make decisions about their own bodies is paramount.

Measuring Impact: It's essential to evaluate the impact of reproductive health education programs rigorously. This evaluation includes assessing how education and access to contraception influence family planning decisions and fertility rates. Monitoring progress helps refine programs and ensures that they continue to meet the needs of communities.

Global Initiatives: Reproductive health education is a global concern, and various international organizations work to promote access to family planning resources and education. These organizations collaborate to advance this critical aspect of population management worldwide, recognizing that family planning is an integral part of sustainable development and a means to address pressing global challenges.

2. Empowering Women and Gender Equality:

Gender equality and women's empowerment are closely linked to lower fertility rates. When women have access to education, economic opportunities, and control over their reproductive choices, they tend to have fewer children.

Education as a Catalyst

Education plays a pivotal role in empowering women and reducing fertility rates. Girls' and women's access to quality education equips them with knowledge and skills, enabling them to make informed decisions about their lives, including family planning. Education often delays the age at which women marry and have children, leading to smaller family sizes.

Economic Empowerment

Economic opportunities for women are essential in the context of population reduction. When women have access to jobs and income-generating activities, they gain greater financial independence. Economic empowerment not only allows women to support their families but also provides an incentive to have fewer children. Initiatives that promote women's entrepreneurship, equal pay, and workforce participation contribute to population reduction.

Reproductive Health Services

Access to reproductive health services, including contraception and maternal healthcare, is a fundamental component of gender equality. When women have control over their reproductive choices and can access essential healthcare services, they can better plan and space their pregnancies. Improving access to these services empowers women to make decisions that lead to lower fertility rates.

Legal Rights and Autonomy

Legal rights and autonomy over one's body are critical aspects of gender equality. Laws and policies that protect women's rights, including the right to choose when and how many children to have, are essential. Legal reforms and advocacy efforts contribute to women's empowerment and population reduction.

Social Norms and Cultural Shifts

Gender norms and cultural practices can influence family size and women's reproductive choices. Efforts to challenge and change these norms can lead to positive shifts in fertility rates. Initiatives that challenge harmful traditional practices and promote equitable gender roles within families and communities contribute to population reduction.

Health and Well-being

The overall health and well-being of women are integral to population reduction. Addressing issues such as maternal mortality, gender-based violence, and women's mental health contributes to healthier and more empowered women who can make choices about their reproductive futures. Comprehensive healthcare and support systems are vital components of gender equality and population management.

Education and Advocacy

Educational campaigns and advocacy efforts play a crucial role in promoting gender equality and women's empowerment. Successful initiatives that have led to positive changes in women's lives and the strategies used to raise awareness and drive social change are essential.

Global Impact

Gender equality and women's empowerment are global concerns, and international organizations and grassroots movements work tirelessly to advance these principles. Global initiatives that focus on women's rights and their connection to sustainable development and population reduction are examined.

Data and Monitoring

Collecting and analyzing data on gender equality indicators and fertility rates is essential for measuring progress. Data-driven approaches help identify areas for improvement and track the impact of gender equality initiatives on population reduction.

Policy and Legislation

Policies and legislation that promote gender equality are crucial components of population reduction. These policies contribute to creating an environment where women can make informed choices about their reproductive futures.

3. Voluntary and Incentivized Measures:

Several countries have implemented voluntary and incentivized measures to promote smaller families within their populations. These measures are designed to provide incentives for individuals and couples who choose to have fewer children. In this section, we'll delve into the ethical considerations and effectiveness of such measures.

Tax Incentives: Some countries offer tax incentives to families with fewer children. These incentives typically result in reduced tax liabilities for families who decide to limit their family size. The rationale behind this approach is to provide financial relief to those who make a conscious choice to have smaller families, which, in turn, can alleviate some of the economic pressures associated with raising children.

Cash Transfers: Another strategy involves providing direct cash transfers to families that maintain a smaller family size. These transfers can serve as financial support for families, particularly those in lower-income brackets. By offering financial incentives, governments aim to encourage family planning decisions that align with population reduction goals.

Benefits and Support: Beyond tax incentives and cash transfers, some countries offer various benefits and support systems to families with fewer children. These benefits may include access to improved healthcare services, education opportunities, or housing assistance. By providing a range of benefits, governments aim to create a supportive environment for individuals and couples who opt for smaller families.

Ethical Considerations: The implementation of voluntary and incentivized measures raises ethical questions and considerations. Critics argue that such measures may infringe on reproductive rights and personal freedoms, as they may pressure individuals and couples into making specific family planning choices. Balancing the desire for population reduction with individual autonomy is a complex ethical challenge that policymakers grapple with.

Effectiveness: Assessing the effectiveness of these measures is essential. Governments and organizations conduct ongoing evaluations to determine whether voluntary and incentivized measures contribute to population reduction goals. Effectiveness varies depending on factors such as the level of incentives, cultural acceptance, and the overall socio-economic context of the country.

International Perspectives: We'll also explore how different countries approach these measures from an international perspective. While some nations have successfully implemented such programs, others may face challenges in their adoption due to cultural, ethical, or political considerations. Understanding the global landscape of voluntary and incentivized measures provides valuable insights into their potential impact on reducing population growth.

By examining the ethical dimensions and effectiveness of these voluntary and incentivized measures, we aim to shed light on the complex choices governments make in their efforts to address population challenges while respecting individual rights and autonomy.

4. Education and Awareness:

Education and awareness campaigns are powerful tools in shaping family size decisions and influencing population growth. In this section, we will explore the role of education and awareness programs in reducing population growth.

Informing Individuals and Communities: Educational campaigns provide individuals and communities with valuable information about the environmental, social, and economic benefits of smaller families. They explain how smaller families can contribute to reduced resource consumption, lower carbon footprints, and improved overall well-being. By informing people about these advantages, educational initiatives empower them to make informed family planning choices.

Promoting Reproductive Health: Beyond general awareness, education programs often emphasize the importance of reproductive health. They offer guidance on contraception methods, family planning options, and the significance of spacing pregnancies. Access to comprehensive reproductive health education ensures that individuals and couples have the knowledge and tools to make choices that align with their family size preferences.

Environmental Sustainability: Environmental education is a key component of these campaigns, highlighting the connection between family size and environmental sustainability. Education programs stress how reducing population growth can help mitigate the depletion of natural resources, curb habitat destruction, and combat climate change. Understanding the environmental implications of family size is instrumental in encouraging sustainable choices.

Social and Economic Benefits: Education and awareness initiatives also underscore the social and economic benefits of smaller families. They emphasize how reduced family sizes can lead to better access to education and healthcare for children, improved economic opportunities for parents, and enhanced overall family well-being.

These campaigns aim to dispel misconceptions and provide evidence-based information.

Global and Local Initiatives: We will explore both global and local perspectives on educational campaigns. Internationally, organizations and governments collaborate on awareness programs that address population challenges. Locally tailored initiatives consider cultural contexts, societal norms, and regional priorities to effectively reach communities and individuals.

Measuring Impact: Evaluating the impact of education and awareness programs is crucial. Governments and organizations conduct assessments to determine the effectiveness of their campaigns. Metrics may include changes in family size preferences, increased use of contraception, and shifts in public perception regarding the benefits of smaller families.

Community Engagement: Successful educational campaigns often involve community engagement strategies. They encourage dialogue, provide forums for discussion, and foster support networks for individuals and couples. Community involvement helps break down barriers to open conversations about family planning.

By delving into the multifaceted role of education and awareness programs, we aim to understand how they contribute to reduced population growth. These initiatives empower individuals with knowledge and offer the tools they need to make choices aligned with environmental sustainability, social well-being, and economic stability.

5. Access to Healthcare:

Access to healthcare, particularly maternal and child healthcare, plays a crucial role in influencing family size decisions and ultimately reducing population growth. In this section, we will delve into the importance of improved access to healthcare and how it contributes to smaller family sizes.

Child Mortality and Family Size: One of the key factors affecting family size decisions is child mortality. When access to healthcare is limited, parents may have larger families as a form of insurance against the higher likelihood of child mortality. Improved access to healthcare, especially for maternal and child health services, reduces child mortality rates. As parents gain confidence that their children will survive to adulthood, they tend to have fewer children.

Maternal Health: Adequate maternal healthcare is critical for both the well-being of mothers and influencing family size. Access to prenatal care, safe deliveries, and postnatal care not only ensures the health of mothers but also contributes to healthier children. When mothers receive quality healthcare during pregnancy and childbirth, the chances of child survival increase, impacting family size decisions.

Child Health Services: Healthcare services tailored to children, including vaccinations, preventive care, and treatment of common childhood illnesses, are essential in reducing child mortality. These services contribute to lower child mortality rates, and parents may choose to have smaller families knowing that their children have a higher likelihood of surviving and thriving.

Family Planning Services: Access to family planning services within healthcare systems is a fundamental component of reducing population growth. It allows individuals and couples to make informed decisions about the timing and spacing of their children. When healthcare facilities provide access to contraception and family planning counseling, it empowers people to have the number of children they desire.

Education and Awareness: The role of education and awareness campaigns in healthcare access cannot be understated. These campaigns often promote the benefits of maternal and child healthcare, including its positive impact on family size decisions. They raise awareness about available healthcare services and encourage individuals to seek care for themselves and their children.

Community Outreach: Effective healthcare access extends beyond the physical availability of services. Community outreach programs play a vital role in reaching underserved populations. These programs provide information, facilitate healthcare access, and build trust within communities, especially in remote or marginalized areas.

Measuring Impact: Evaluating the impact of improved healthcare access involves monitoring key indicators such as child mortality rates, maternal health outcomes, and the utilization of family planning services. Data-driven assessments help healthcare providers and policymakers refine their strategies to enhance access further.

Global Efforts: The section will also explore global efforts to improve healthcare access, including initiatives led by international organizations, governments, and non-governmental organizations. Collaboration at the international level is essential to address healthcare disparities and ensure that healthcare access is a global priority.

By understanding the multifaceted role of improved healthcare access, we gain insights into how it contributes to smaller family sizes. This, in turn, has a positive impact on reducing population growth rates while promoting the health and well-being of individuals and communities.

6. Delayed Marriage and Parenthood:

Cultural shifts and economic pressures have ushered in a trend of delayed marriage and parenthood in many societies. In this section, we will delve into how these trends impact population growth and the broader societal implications.

Changing Social Norms: Over the past few decades, societal norms around marriage and parenthood have evolved significantly. In many parts of the world, there has been a departure from traditional expectations of early marriage and starting a family soon after. Factors contributing to this shift include a greater emphasis on individual choice, educational pursuits, and career aspirations. These changing social norms influence the timing of marriage and parenthood.

Educational Pursuits: Access to education, particularly for women, has expanded substantially. As a result, individuals are pursuing higher levels of education and training, which often leads to later entry into the workforce and delayed family planning. Educational opportunities contribute to delaying marriage and parenthood and impact population growth.

Career Considerations: Economic pressures and career considerations play a pivotal role in the decision to delay marriage and parenthood. Young adults are increasingly focusing on establishing their careers, achieving financial stability, and securing a stable living environment before starting a family. Economic factors contribute to delayed family planning.

Family Planning: Delayed marriage and parenthood are often associated with family planning. Couples who choose to wait before having children tend to engage in family planning practices, such as contraception and fertility awareness. Family planning plays a role in delaying parenthood and its implications for population growth.

Social and Demographic Effects: The shift towards delayed marriage and parenthood has demographic consequences. It can lead to a temporary reduction in birth rates, which, when sustained, contributes to lower population growth rates. Delayed family formation impacts demographic trends and population projections.

Policy Considerations: Policymakers often consider the implications of delayed marriage and parenthood when crafting family planning and social policies. In some cases, governments may provide support for family planning services, parental leave, and child care to accommodate the needs of couples who choose to delay parenthood. Policy addresses the challenges and opportunities associated with this trend.

Cultural Variations: Cultural factors play a significant role in determining the acceptable age for marriage and parenthood. Cultural variations in attitudes towards delayed family formation contribute to demographic diversity.

Global Perspectives: This section will also provide a global perspective by examining how delayed marriage and parenthood trends differ across countries and regions. Cultural, economic, and social factors vary widely, leading to distinct patterns of family formation.

By understanding the complex interplay of cultural shifts, economic factors, and changing social norms, we gain insights into how delayed marriage and parenthood impact population growth. This knowledge is essential for policymakers and researchers striving to address demographic challenges and plan for the future.

7. Urbanization:

This section offers a comprehensive view of urbanization by considering how trends in urbanization differ across countries and regions, and how these differences shape demographic patterns on a global scale.

Regional Variation: Urbanization is not a uniform process; it varies significantly from one region to another. In some parts of the world, urbanization has been rapid and transformative, with large segments of the population moving to cities. In contrast, other regions may experience slower urbanization or have unique urban development patterns. This section will explore these regional variations.

Factors Driving Urbanization: To understand the global picture, it's crucial to examine the factors that drive urbanization in different regions. Economic opportunities, industrialization, rural-to-urban migration, and government policies all play varying roles in shaping urbanization trends. We will discuss how these factors contribute to demographic shifts.

Urbanization and Demographic Transition: Urbanization is closely linked to the demographic transition, which involves a shift from high birth and death rates to lower birth and death rates. Understanding how urbanization fits into this transition is key to analyzing global demographic patterns.

Urbanization and Population Growth: Urbanization can have profound effects on population growth. It often leads to a decline in fertility rates as families adapt to urban lifestyles, with smaller family sizes becoming the norm. By exploring these dynamics, we can gain insights into the role of urbanization in moderating population growth worldwide.

Challenges and Opportunities: Urbanization presents both challenges and opportunities for societies. It can strain resources and infrastructure in rapidly growing cities, but it can also drive economic development and innovation. We will delve into the implications of these challenges and opportunities on demographic patterns.

Urbanization and Sustainability: As the world grapples with sustainability issues, understanding the environmental impact of urbanization is crucial. Urban areas tend to be more resource-intensive, and their growth can have significant environmental consequences. We will discuss how urbanization trends affect global sustainability efforts.

Case Studies: To illustrate these global perspectives, we will include case studies of countries or regions that have experienced distinct urbanization trajectories. These case studies will highlight the unique challenges and successes associated with urbanization in different parts of the world.

Policy Implications: Policymakers and governments worldwide are tasked with addressing the effects of urbanization on demographics and society. This section will explore the policy responses and initiatives implemented in various regions to manage urbanization's impact on population dynamics.

By examining urbanization from a global perspective, we aim to provide a nuanced understanding of its role in shaping demographic patterns and its significance in the context of global population dynamics. This understanding is essential for policymakers, researchers, and organizations working to address the challenges and opportunities presented by urbanization on a global scale.

8. Ethical Considerations:

Throughout this exploration, we will continuously discuss the ethical dimensions of population reduction strategies. Ethical considerations include individual rights, reproductive autonomy, social justice, and the potential for coercion or discrimination in implementing such strategies.

Individual Rights: At the heart of ethical considerations is the concept of individual rights. These rights encompass the autonomy and freedom of individuals to make choices about their reproductive health and family size. It is crucial to respect and protect these rights while implementing population reduction strategies. This includes ensuring that individuals have access to comprehensive information about family planning options and can make decisions free from coercion or undue influence.

Reproductive Autonomy: Reproductive autonomy is closely linked to individual rights and encompasses the ability of individuals or couples to make informed decisions about family planning and reproduction. In an ethical framework, population reduction strategies should enhance reproductive autonomy by providing individuals with the resources and support they need to make choices that align with their values and goals. This includes access to a range of contraceptive methods and family planning services.

Social Justice: Ethical considerations extend to questions of social justice. It is essential to examine how population reduction strategies can impact different societal groups. For instance, these strategies should not disproportionately burden vulnerable or marginalized populations. Ethical practices demand that the benefits and burdens of these strategies are distributed fairly and equitably. This involves conducting thorough equity assessments and addressing disparities in access to healthcare and family planning services.

Coercion and Discrimination: Ensuring that population reduction strategies are implemented without coercion or discrimination is paramount. It is unethical to force individuals or communities to adopt specific family planning practices against their will. Moreover, these strategies should not discriminate against certain groups based on factors like ethnicity, gender, or socioeconomic status. Ethical guidelines must include safeguards to prevent any form of coercion or discrimination.

Informed Consent: Ethical practices require informed consent, implying that individuals should have access to accurate information about population reduction measures. They should also be able to make choices based on this information without any pressure or manipulation. This entails robust educational campaigns that provide clear and unbiased information about family planning options, as well as ensuring that individuals have the capacity to understand and make informed decisions.

Cultural Sensitivity: Cultural values and norms significantly influence reproductive decisions. Ethical considerations include respecting cultural diversity while implementing population reduction strategies. This means tailoring interventions to be culturally sensitive, acknowledging and respecting local practices, and engaging with communities to ensure that strategies align with their values and beliefs.

Cultural competency is essential for ethical and effective interventions.

Transparency and Accountability: Maintaining transparency and accountability in the design and implementation of population reduction strategies is vital. Ethical frameworks demand clear guidelines, oversight mechanisms, and avenues for redress in case of any ethical violations. Transparency ensures that individuals and communities can trust the process and outcomes of these strategies, while accountability holds responsible parties to ethical standards.

Balancing Ethical Concerns: Striking a balance between addressing ethical concerns associated with population reduction and addressing global challenges such as environmental sustainability is a complex task. Ethical frameworks require policymakers and stakeholders to carefully consider the trade-offs and ethical dilemmas involved. This includes conducting ethical impact assessments and engaging in transparent decision-making processes.

Global Cooperation: Given the global nature of population dynamics, ethical considerations extend to international cooperation and agreements. Ethical frameworks emphasize the importance of collaboration among nations to address population-related challenges ethically and effectively. This includes sharing best practices, resources, and knowledge while respecting the sovereignty and self-determination of nations.

By considering these ethical dimensions, policymakers and stakeholders can develop and implement population reduction strategies that uphold individual rights, promote social justice, and respect diverse cultural values while addressing global challenges.

9. Global Perspectives:

Approaching the topic of population reduction requires a nuanced understanding of diverse perspectives from around the world. It is crucial to acknowledge that different regions and nations may have unique cultural, social, and economic contexts that influence their stance on population-related issues. Population reduction strategies should be designed and implemented with sensitivity to these global perspectives.

Respect for Cultural Diversity: One of the key aspects of global perspectives is the recognition and respect for cultural diversity. What may be considered an acceptable or ethical population reduction strategy in one culture may not align with the values and beliefs of another. Ethical considerations demand that strategies respect and honor the cultural norms and traditions of each community. This involves engaging with local stakeholders, including community leaders and elders, to ensure that initiatives are culturally sensitive.

Ethical and Human Rights Implications: Population reduction strategies have profound ethical and human rights implications. These implications touch on issues of reproductive autonomy, individual rights, social justice, and equity. When exploring population reduction strategies, it is essential to delve into how these strategies align with international human rights principles and ethical guidelines. This includes ensuring that individuals are not coerced into family planning practices and that they have access to a full range of family planning options.

Equity and Disparities: Global perspectives also encompass the consideration of global equity and disparities. Some regions may experience rapid population growth, while others may face declining populations. Ethical frameworks call for strategies that address these disparities and ensure that the benefits of population reduction are equitably distributed. This involves examining the root causes of population disparities, such as unequal access to education and healthcare, and developing strategies that promote equity.

Cross-Cultural Dialogue: Engaging in cross-cultural dialogue and collaboration is a fundamental aspect of addressing global population issues. It allows for the sharing of best practices, lessons learned, and innovative approaches from different parts of the world. By delving into these cross-cultural dialogues, we aim to foster a deeper understanding of the complexities and nuances of population reduction efforts across diverse regions.

Local Ownership and Participation: Effective population reduction strategies should prioritize local ownership and participation. Communities must have a voice in the development and implementation of these strategies. Global perspectives emphasize the importance of community engagement, empowerment, and the inclusion of diverse voices in decision-making processes. This ensures that strategies are contextually relevant and ethically sound.

International Cooperation: Given the global nature of population dynamics, international cooperation is crucial. Ethical frameworks call for collaboration among nations to address population-related challenges collectively. This involves the sharing of resources, knowledge, and expertise to develop and implement ethical and effective strategies. It also respects the sovereignty and self-determination of each nation while recognizing the interconnectedness of global population trends.

Sustainable Development Goals (SDGs): Global perspectives should align with the United Nations Sustainable Development Goals (SDGs), particularly Goal 3 (Good Health and Well-being), Goal 4 (Quality Education), Goal 5 (Gender Equality), and Goal 10 (Reduced Inequality). These goals provide a global framework for addressing population-related challenges ethically and sustainably.

By delving into these global perspectives, we aim to provide a comprehensive overview of the complex landscape of population reduction expectations and initiatives. It is through a deep understanding of diverse global viewpoints that effective, ethical, and culturally sensitive population reduction strategies can be developed and implemented to address the challenges of our rapidly changing world.

Chapter 10: Pandemics and the Future

Section 1: Projected Virus Impact

Explore the potential impact of viruses in the future.

Projected Virus Impact:

Understanding the potential impact of viruses in the future is essential for preparedness and mitigation efforts. Viruses have been a persistent threat to human health throughout history, and their impact can vary significantly based on factors such as virus type, transmission dynamics, healthcare infrastructure, and global interconnectedness.

Virus Type and Characteristics: The nature of the virus itself is a pivotal factor in determining its impact on human health and society. Viruses can range from relatively benign, causing mild illnesses like the common cold, to highly lethal, such as the Ebola virus. Delving into the specific characteristics of a virus includes examining its genetic makeup, modes of transmission, incubation periods, and mutation rates. For instance, viruses that mutate rapidly may pose challenges for vaccine development and treatment, while those with longer incubation periods may spread more stealthily in a population.

Transmission Dynamics: Understanding how viruses spread within communities is crucial for assessing their potential impact. This involves delving into the dynamics of transmission, including the mechanisms by which viruses move from one host to another. Airborne viruses can spread quickly, especially in densely populated areas, while viruses transmitted primarily through direct contact may have a slower rate of transmission. Factors like population density, social interactions, and travel patterns all play into transmission dynamics, influencing how widely and rapidly a virus can propagate.

Healthcare Infrastructure: The resilience and capacity of healthcare systems are fundamental in mitigating the impact of viral outbreaks. Delving into healthcare infrastructure involves examining aspects like the availability of medical facilities, trained healthcare personnel, diagnostic tools, treatments, and hospital bed capacity. For instance, regions with well-equipped healthcare systems are better positioned to handle outbreaks, provide timely treatment, and minimize the strain on healthcare resources.

Global Interconnectedness: The modern world is characterized by extensive global interconnectedness, facilitating the rapid spread of infectious diseases. Delving into this aspect involves analyzing international travel patterns, trade routes, and migration flows. Air travel, in particular, has made it possible for viruses to traverse vast distances in a short time. Understanding the extent of global interconnectedness helps predict how far and fast a virus may disseminate, making it a critical factor in assessing its potential impact.

Zoonotic Potential: Zoonotic diseases, which originate in animals and jump to humans, have been responsible for numerous pandemics. Delving into the zoonotic potential of viruses includes examining factors like wildlife trade, habitat encroachment, and the dynamics of interspecies transmission. By understanding these dynamics, we can identify potential sources of future viral outbreaks and take preventive measures.

Antibiotic Resistance: In addition to viral threats, bacterial infections with antibiotic resistance are becoming increasingly concerning. Delving into this issue entails examining the factors contributing to antibiotic resistance, such as the overuse of antibiotics in healthcare and agriculture. The potential for bacterial infections, often secondary to viral illnesses, to become resistant to treatment complicates the response to pandemics.

Vaccination Coverage: Vaccines are a powerful tool in reducing the impact of viral diseases. Delving into vaccination coverage involves assessing the availability of vaccines, vaccination rates, and vaccine hesitancy. Additionally, ongoing research into new vaccines, including those that target emerging viral threats, is essential for preparedness efforts. Understanding vaccination dynamics is vital for planning and executing effective vaccination campaigns.

Public Health Measures: Delving into the effectiveness and acceptability of public health measures, such as quarantine, isolation, and contact tracing, is crucial for pandemic response. These measures can significantly influence the course of an outbreak by reducing transmission rates. Understanding their effectiveness in different contexts and among diverse populations informs strategies for future pandemics.

Global Cooperation: International cooperation is indispensable in addressing global health threats. Delving into this aspect involves evaluating the state of international collaboration mechanisms, data sharing, research coordination, and response efforts. Strong global cooperation enhances our collective ability to respond effectively to viral challenges, as evidenced by initiatives like COVAX during the COVID-19 pandemic.

By delving into these multifaceted factors, we gain a holistic understanding of the potential impact of viruses in the future. This knowledge equips us to make informed decisions, allocate resources effectively, and implement measures that can mitigate the impact of viral outbreaks on human health and society.

Emerging and Re-emerging Diseases:

The future is likely to witness the emergence and re-emergence of infectious diseases caused by both known and novel viruses. Factors such as environmental changes, increased human-animal interactions, and global travel contribute to the spread of viruses. Exploring the potential scenarios of emerging diseases helps in early detection and response.

Environmental Changes: Environmental factors play a significant role in the emergence of infectious diseases. Changes in climate, land use, and ecosystems can impact disease dynamics. For instance, rising temperatures can expand the geographical range of disease-carrying mosquitoes, potentially exposing new populations to diseases like malaria and dengue. Understanding these links between environmental shifts and disease prevalence is crucial for early detection and adaptation strategies.

Human-Animal Interactions: Increased human encroachment into natural habitats and interactions with wildlife heighten the risk of zoonotic disease transmission. By studying human-animal interactions, we examine behaviors like hunting, trade, and consumption of wild animals, which can lead to zoonotic spillover events. Identifying high-risk behaviors is essential for predicting and preventing disease outbreaks.

Global Travel and Trade: Modern global travel and trade networks facilitate the rapid spread of infectious diseases. Analyzing international travel patterns, cargo shipments, and population movements across borders is crucial. Air travel, in particular, can expedite the global dissemination of pathogens. Understanding these pathways of disease transmission informs measures like border controls, quarantine protocols, and international health regulations.

Disease Surveillance and Early Detection: Early detection of emerging diseases is essential for swift response and containment. Disease surveillance involves assessing the effectiveness of monitoring systems, laboratory capacities, and information sharing mechanisms. Advanced technologies, such as genomic sequencing and real-time data analysis, aid in early detection efforts. Strengthening global and regional surveillance networks enhances our ability to identify and respond to outbreaks promptly.

Research and Vaccine Development: Ongoing research on known pathogens and the development of vaccines and treatments are critical in combating emerging diseases. This research includes studying the genetic makeup of viruses, potential reservoirs, and host-pathogen interactions. Vaccine development efforts are essential for preparedness. Anticipating potential viral scenarios guides research priorities and accelerates the development of countermeasures.

Community Engagement and Risk Communication: Effective communication with communities is vital for outbreak response and prevention. Strategies for community engagement involve assessing public awareness, trust in health authorities, and the dissemination of accurate information during outbreaks. Building trust and ensuring that communities are informed about disease risks and preventive measures are essential components of pandemic preparedness.

By exploring these multifaceted factors related to emerging and re-emerging diseases, we can better anticipate and respond to the evolving landscape of infectious diseases in the future. This comprehensive understanding enables us to implement proactive measures, improve preparedness, and ultimately reduce the impact of emerging diseases on global health.

Viral Evolution:

Viruses are known for their ability to evolve rapidly. Understanding the evolutionary dynamics of viruses, including antigenic variation and the development of resistance mechanisms, is crucial for vaccine development and treatment strategies.

Antigenic Variation: Viruses exhibit antigenic variation, a process where they change their surface proteins over time. This variation can be gradual or abrupt and is often driven by natural selection. Antigenic variation is particularly relevant for influenza viruses, which frequently undergo changes in their surface antigens. Understanding these shifts is essential for updating seasonal influenza vaccines to match the most prevalent strains.

Resistance Mechanisms: As viruses are exposed to antiviral drugs or immune responses, they can develop resistance mechanisms. This phenomenon has been observed in diseases like HIV and hepatitis C, where viral strains resistant to standard treatments can emerge. Investigating these mechanisms involves studying viral replication and genetic changes that confer resistance. Developing strategies to counteract resistance is critical for effective treatments.

Host-Pathogen Interactions: Viral evolution is deeply intertwined with host-pathogen interactions. By studying the interactions between viruses and their hosts, researchers gain insights into how viruses adapt to their environment. This includes examining how viruses evade the host's immune system, establish persistent infections, or shift from animal reservoirs to human hosts. Understanding these dynamics aids in predicting the potential for spillover events and disease emergence.

Vaccine Development Challenges: Viral evolution presents challenges for vaccine development. Vaccines are typically designed to target specific viral antigens, but when these antigens change due to viral evolution, vaccines may become less effective. This is a concern with viruses like HIV, where rapid antigenic variation has hindered vaccine development. Researchers need to explore innovative vaccine strategies, such as mosaic vaccines or broadly neutralizing antibodies, to address these challenges.

Surveillance for Viral Variants: Monitoring viral evolution through surveillance efforts is essential. Surveillance involves collecting and analyzing viral samples from various sources, including patients, animals, and the environment. This process helps identify new variants, track their spread, and assess their potential impact on public health. Genomic sequencing plays a crucial role in characterizing viral diversity and evolution.

One Health Approach: Viral evolution is closely linked to broader ecological and One Health concepts. Recognizing the interconnectedness of human, animal, and environmental health is essential for understanding viral evolution. By studying viral dynamics in ecosystems and the human-animal interface, we can anticipate potential spillover events and take preventive measures.

Ethical Considerations: As we delve into the complexities of viral evolution, ethical considerations come into play. Questions related to the responsible use of antiviral drugs, the potential impact of resistance on vulnerable populations, and equitable access to treatments must be explored. Additionally, ethical discussions encompass the balance between surveillance for public health and individual privacy rights.

By exploring these aspects of viral evolution, we gain a deeper understanding of the dynamic nature of viruses and the challenges they pose to public health. This knowledge informs strategies for vaccine development, treatment approaches, and proactive measures to mitigate the impact of viral evolution on global health.

Pandemic Preparedness:

The lessons learned from past pandemics, such as the Spanish flu of 1918, the H1N1 influenza pandemic of 2009, and the COVID-19 pandemic, inform our approach to future virus impact. Pandemic preparedness involves examining the strengths and weaknesses of healthcare systems, the availability of vaccines and antiviral drugs, and international cooperation in response efforts.

Historical Perspectives: To understand how future viruses might impact us, it's essential to look back at significant pandemics in history. Events like the Spanish flu of 1918, the H1N1 influenza pandemic of 2009, and the ongoing COVID-19 pandemic have left indelible marks on public health. By analyzing these historical pandemics, we gain insights into the factors that contribute to their emergence, transmission, and containment.

Healthcare System Resilience: One of the critical aspects of pandemic preparedness is evaluating the resilience of healthcare systems. This includes assessing the capacity of hospitals, healthcare personnel, and medical supply chains to respond to a surge in cases. Lessons from previous pandemics have highlighted the importance of having robust healthcare infrastructure and surge capacity to handle emergencies effectively.

Vaccine and Antiviral Availability: The availability of vaccines and antiviral drugs plays a pivotal role in pandemic preparedness. Developing vaccines and treatments that can be rapidly deployed is a priority. Understanding the processes involved in vaccine development, regulatory approvals, and distribution logistics is crucial for ensuring timely access to effective countermeasures.

International Cooperation: Viruses do not respect national borders, making international cooperation a cornerstone of pandemic response. Examining the level of collaboration between countries, sharing of data and resources, and adherence to international health regulations is essential. Global preparedness efforts require coordination and solidarity among nations to mount an effective response to emerging viruses.

Surveillance and Early Warning Systems: Pandemic preparedness also involves enhancing surveillance and early warning systems. This includes monitoring for unusual patterns of disease, conducting genomic sequencing to identify emerging variants, and setting up mechanisms for rapid information sharing. These systems enable early detection and response to potential threats.

Community Engagement: Engaging communities in pandemic preparedness is critical. People need to be aware of the risks, understand preventive measures, and know how to access healthcare services during a pandemic. Communication strategies that disseminate accurate information and combat misinformation are essential components of preparedness efforts.

Ethical Considerations: As we contemplate the impact of future viruses, ethical considerations come into play. These include questions about equitable access to vaccines and treatments, the allocation of limited resources during a pandemic, and the protection of vulnerable populations. Ethical frameworks guide decision-making in complex situations.

By examining these facets of pandemic preparedness, we can better position ourselves to respond effectively to future virus impacts. Drawing from historical experiences, bolstering healthcare systems, fostering international collaboration, and engaging communities are all essential components of a proactive approach to pandemic readiness.

Vaccine Development and Distribution:

The development, testing, and distribution of vaccines play a vital role in mitigating the impact of viral diseases. Exploring the challenges and innovations in vaccine development, including mRNA vaccine technology, can shed light on our ability to respond effectively to future viral threats.

Innovations in Vaccine Development: A crucial aspect of countering future viral threats is the continuous innovation in vaccine development. This involves not only refining traditional vaccine approaches but also exploring cutting-edge technologies. The emergence of mRNA vaccine technology has marked a significant milestone in our ability to respond rapidly to novel viruses. By examining these innovative approaches, we gain insight into the potential for developing effective vaccines against a wide range of pathogens.

Challenges in Vaccine Distribution: Developing vaccines is only part of the equation; ensuring equitable distribution is equally vital. Examining the challenges involved in the distribution process is crucial for addressing disparities in access to vaccines. Factors such as supply chain logistics, cold storage requirements, and global distribution networks all play a role in determining how effectively vaccines can reach those in need.

Global Vaccination Efforts: In an interconnected world, addressing viral threats necessitates a global approach to vaccination. Understanding international initiatives, collaborations, and organizations dedicated to vaccine distribution is essential. Examining the roles played by organizations like COVAX in ensuring vaccine access for low- and middle-income countries underscores the importance of coordinated efforts in a global context.

Vaccine Hesitancy and Communication: Vaccine hesitancy poses a significant challenge to vaccination efforts. Exploring the factors that contribute to vaccine hesitancy, including misinformation and distrust, allows us to develop targeted communication strategies. Effective communication is crucial for building public confidence in vaccines and encouraging widespread vaccination, which is essential for achieving herd immunity and controlling future pandemics.

Emergency Use Authorization: The concept of emergency use authorization (EUA) for vaccines has gained prominence during the COVID-19 pandemic. Delving into the criteria and processes involved in granting EUA provides insights into the regulatory mechanisms that facilitate rapid vaccine deployment during emergencies. Understanding these mechanisms is critical for expediting vaccine access when needed most.

Ethical Considerations in Vaccine Deployment: The equitable and ethical deployment of vaccines is a paramount concern. Examining ethical frameworks for vaccine allocation, especially when resources are limited, helps guide decision-making in challenging situations. Ethical considerations encompass issues like prioritizing vulnerable populations, addressing vaccine nationalism, and ensuring that no one is left behind in vaccination efforts.

By exploring these facets of vaccine development and distribution, we gain a comprehensive understanding of the complexities involved in countering viral threats. Innovations in vaccine technologies, equitable distribution strategies, and ethical considerations are all integral components of a robust response to future viral diseases.

Global Health Security:

Viruses do not respect national borders, highlighting the importance of global health security. The mechanisms of international collaboration, data sharing, and early warning systems can help us understand how the global community can work together to prevent and respond to viral outbreaks.

International Collaboration: The interconnected nature of our world underscores the significance of international collaboration in safeguarding global health. Understanding the mechanisms through which countries cooperate, share data, and pool resources in response to viral outbreaks is essential. Such collaboration ensures that nations can collectively address emerging threats and deploy resources where they are most needed.

Data Sharing and Surveillance: Effective global health security relies on robust data sharing and surveillance systems. Examining the methods by which countries and international organizations collect, analyze, and share epidemiological data can shed light on the early detection of viral outbreaks. Early warning systems that monitor unusual disease patterns and trends are instrumental in averting potential pandemics.

Pandemic Preparedness Frameworks: Delving into the frameworks and strategies established by international bodies, such as the World Health Organization (WHO), can provide insights into pandemic preparedness. These frameworks encompass guidelines for response coordination, resource allocation, and communication protocols among nations. Understanding how these frameworks function ensures a coordinated and efficient global response to viral threats.

Humanitarian Assistance and Support: In the wake of viral outbreaks, humanitarian assistance often plays a vital role. Exploring the ways in which the international community offers support to affected regions, including medical supplies, personnel, and financial aid, highlights the collaborative efforts aimed at minimizing the impact of pandemics on vulnerable populations.

Capacity Building and Resilience: Building the capacity of nations, particularly those with limited resources, is a cornerstone of global health security. Investigating initiatives that strengthen healthcare infrastructure, laboratory capabilities, and healthcare workforce training underscores the importance of preparedness. These capacity-building efforts enhance a nation's ability to respond effectively to outbreaks.

Multilateral Agreements: International agreements and treaties are instrumental in promoting global health security. Examining these agreements, such as the International Health Regulations (IHR), provides insights into the legal frameworks governing pandemic response. Understanding the obligations and responsibilities outlined in these agreements fosters accountability and compliance among nations.

By exploring these aspects of global health security, we gain a comprehensive understanding of the collaborative efforts required to prevent, detect, and respond to viral outbreaks on a global scale. International cooperation, data sharing, preparedness frameworks, and capacity-building initiatives are all integral components of a resilient global health security system.

One Health Approach:

The One Health approach recognizes the interconnectedness of human, animal, and environmental health. Understanding how zoonotic diseases (those transmitted from animals to humans) can lead to pandemics involves exploring the dynamics of wildlife populations, livestock farming, and human-animal interfaces.

Interconnected Health Realms: The One Health approach embodies the recognition that the health of humans, animals, and the environment is intricately interconnected. Examining this approach involves understanding the dynamics that link these realms. Zoonotic diseases, which can leap from animals to humans, highlight the significance of wildlife populations, livestock farming, and the interfaces where human and animal activities intersect.

Zoonotic Disease Transmission: Within the One Health framework, exploring the mechanisms of zoonotic disease transmission unveils the complex interplay between different species. Investigating how diseases like avian influenza,

Ebola, and coronaviruses originate in wildlife and spill over into human populations underscores the importance of wildlife management and surveillance.

Wildlife Reservoirs: Many zoonotic viruses find their natural reservoirs in wildlife populations. Understanding the behaviors and habitats of these reservoir species, such as bats and rodents, provides insights into the potential sources of future pandemics. Research into wildlife health and ecology is essential for identifying high-risk areas and implementing preventive measures.

Livestock Farming and Zoonoses: Livestock farming represents a significant interface between humans and animals. Exploring the dynamics of livestock production, including intensive farming practices, antibiotic use, and livestock trade, helps pinpoint areas where zoonotic diseases may emerge. Sustainable and responsible livestock management practices are crucial for minimizing the risk of zoonotic transmission.

Human-Wildlife Conflict: As human populations expand into natural habitats, conflicts between humans and wildlife can escalate. Investigating the consequences of such conflicts, including the displacement of wildlife and changes in behavior, can shed light on the potential for disease transmission. Strategies for mitigating human-wildlife conflicts are essential for reducing zoonotic disease risks.

Environmental Impact: The One Health approach also considers the environmental factors that influence disease transmission. Examining how deforestation, climate change, and habitat degradation affect the distribution of wildlife and their pathogens is integral. This understanding underscores the importance of sustainable environmental practices in preventing pandemics.

By exploring these facets of the One Health approach, we gain a comprehensive understanding of the interconnectedness of human, animal, and environmental health. Recognizing the potential sources and pathways of zoonotic diseases is vital for early detection and mitigation, ultimately contributing to global pandemic preparedness and response efforts.

Social and Economic Impacts:

Viral outbreaks have far-reaching social and economic consequences. The potential societal and economic impacts of future pandemics can inform policy decisions and strategies for risk mitigation.

Widespread Disruption: The occurrence of viral outbreaks can lead to profound disruptions in society and the economy. These disruptions encompass a wide range of aspects, including but not limited to school closures, travel restrictions, interruptions in the supply chain, and a significant strain on healthcare systems.

Healthcare System Strain: The impact on healthcare systems during a pandemic is substantial. This includes the surge in patients requiring medical attention, especially those in need of intensive care. Assessing the readiness and capacity of healthcare systems to manage such surges, including the availability of critical resources like ventilators and personal protective equipment, is a critical aspect of pandemic preparedness.

Economic Resilience: Viral outbreaks can trigger a chain reaction of economic effects. These effects encompass various facets, including how businesses adapt to reduced demand, disruptions in production and distribution, and shifts in consumer behavior. Analyzing the ability of economies to withstand such shocks and developing strategies for maintaining economic stability during a pandemic is of paramount importance.

Social Distancing Measures: Pandemics often necessitate the implementation of social distancing measures like lockdowns and quarantines. Understanding the effectiveness of these measures in curbing the spread of the virus and comprehending their socio-economic costs and benefits is crucial for decision-making during future outbreaks.

Education Disruption: The education sector experiences significant disruption during pandemics, primarily due to school closures. These disruptions impact students' learning, social development, and overall well-being. Investigating the consequences of disrupted education involves considerations of alternative learning methods, challenges related to the digital divide, and the long-term effects on educational outcomes.

Labor Market Dynamics: Pandemics have profound implications for labor markets. These implications encompass various aspects, including job losses, shifts in remote work trends, and the resilience of different industries. Analyzing the dynamics of labor markets during pandemics provides insights into workforce adaptability and may necessitate strategies for supporting affected workers.

Social Inequalities: It's crucial to recognize that pandemics often exacerbate existing social inequalities. This involves analyzing how vulnerable populations, including marginalized communities and those with limited access to healthcare, bear a disproportionate burden during outbreaks. Addressing these disparities and ensuring equitable access to resources are integral components of effective pandemic response and preparedness.

By considering the potential societal and economic impacts of future pandemics in this comprehensive manner, we can better anticipate challenges and proactively develop strategies to mitigate adverse effects. Preparedness efforts should encompass both immediate healthcare responses and broader socio-economic considerations to ensure resilience in the face of viral threats.

Behavioral Factors:

Human behavior plays a significant role in virus transmission. Exploring behavioral factors, such as vaccine hesitancy, adherence to public health guidelines, and information dissemination, can help shape public health interventions and communication strategies.

Vaccine Hesitancy: One of the critical behavioral factors influencing virus transmission is vaccine hesitancy. Understanding the reasons behind individuals' reluctance to get vaccinated is essential for developing targeted interventions.

Factors contributing to vaccine hesitancy may include concerns about vaccine safety, mistrust of healthcare systems, or misinformation circulating through various media channels. Effective strategies to address vaccine hesitancy involve clear and transparent communication, building trust in healthcare institutions, and providing evidence-based information to address concerns.

Adherence to Public Health Guidelines: Compliance with public health guidelines is vital in controlling virus spread. Analyzing the factors that influence individuals' adherence to guidelines, such as mask-wearing, physical distancing, and hand hygiene, is crucial. This involves considering behavioral drivers like risk perception, social norms, and the perceived efficacy of preventive measures. Tailoring communication strategies to promote guideline adherence, addressing misconceptions, and fostering a sense of collective responsibility are essential components of public health interventions.

Information Dissemination: The way information is disseminated during a pandemic greatly affects public perception and behavior. Investigating information sources, the role of social media, and the spread of misinformation helps shape effective communication strategies. Providing accurate, timely, and accessible information through trusted channels is essential for combating misinformation and ensuring that individuals make informed decisions regarding their health and safety.

Community Engagement: Engaging communities is a fundamental approach to influencing behavior during a pandemic. Recognizing the role of communities in disseminating information, supporting vulnerable individuals, and fostering a sense of solidarity is crucial. Strategies for community engagement may involve grassroots initiatives, partnerships with local organizations, and involving community leaders in communication efforts. Empowering communities to take an active role in pandemic response contributes to more effective behavioral outcomes.

Psychological Factors: Pandemics can induce various psychological responses, including fear, anxiety, and stress. Understanding the psychological impact of a pandemic on individuals and communities is essential for providing mental health support and designing interventions that address these challenges. Psychosocial support, access to mental health services, and resilience-building strategies contribute to healthier behavioral responses during and after a pandemic.

This understanding informs the design of public health interventions and communication strategies that align with individuals' needs, perceptions, and behaviors, ultimately contributing to more effective pandemic management.

Ethical Considerations:

Pandemic response involves ethical considerations, including the allocation of limited resources, equity in vaccine distribution, and individual rights versus public health measures. Examining these ethical dilemmas is essential for making informed decisions during a pandemic.

Allocation of Limited Resources: Ethical dilemmas arise when healthcare resources become scarce during a pandemic. This includes situations where there are not enough ventilators, hospital beds, or medical supplies to meet the needs of all patients. Healthcare professionals and policymakers must make difficult decisions about how to allocate these limited resources. Ethical frameworks like utilitarianism, which prioritize the greatest good for the greatest number, may clash with principles of distributive justice that aim for fairness and equitable access to care. Examining these ethical considerations helps guide resource allocation policies that strive to balance the urgent needs of individuals with the broader public good.

Equity in Vaccine Distribution: Ensuring equitable access to vaccines is a paramount ethical concern in pandemic response. Access to vaccines should not be determined by socioeconomic status, nationality, or other factors that can perpetuate health disparities. Ethical principles such as distributive justice and solidarity underscore the importance of fair and equitable vaccine distribution on a global scale. Examining these ethical dilemmas prompts discussions about international cooperation, vaccine donations to low-income countries, and strategies to address vaccine hesitancy among marginalized communities.

Individual Rights vs. Public Health Measures: Balancing individual rights and public health measures can be ethically complex. Pandemic response often involves restrictions on personal freedoms, such as quarantine orders, contact tracing, and mandatory vaccination policies. Ethical considerations include respecting individuals' autonomy and privacy while also safeguarding the well-being of the broader community. Delving into these ethical dimensions helps policymakers strike a balance that upholds individual rights while mitigating the spread of the virus.

Informed Consent: Ethical considerations also extend to the process of informed consent for medical interventions, including vaccines. Ensuring that individuals receive accurate information about the risks and benefits of vaccination is vital. Informed consent is a cornerstone of medical ethics, and it becomes particularly crucial during a pandemic when vaccines are developed and distributed rapidly. Examining these ethical aspects involves designing clear and transparent communication strategies, addressing vaccine hesitancy, and respecting individuals' right to make informed choices about their health.

Transparency and Accountability: Transparency in decision-making and accountability for pandemic response actions are ethical imperatives. Open communication about the rationale behind public health measures, vaccine development, and resource allocation builds trust in healthcare systems. Ethical considerations also encompass accountability for mistakes or shortcomings in pandemic response. An examination of transparency and accountability helps ensure that ethical principles are upheld throughout the crisis.

By examining these ethical considerations, we can navigate the complex terrain of pandemic response while upholding fundamental ethical principles. This examination informs the development of policies and strategies that prioritize both individual rights and the collective well-being, contributing to a more ethical and effective pandemic response.

By exploring the potential impact of viruses in the future, we aim to better understand the challenges and opportunities in pandemic preparedness and response. This knowledge is crucial for safeguarding public health, minimizing societal disruption, and ensuring a resilient global response to emerging infectious diseases.

Chapter 11: The Specter of War

Future Regional Conflicts

Discuss the possibility of future large-scale conflicts.

The Shifting Landscape of Conflict:

The possibility of future large-scale conflicts is a topic that demands close examination in a rapidly changing world. The landscape of conflict has evolved significantly over the years. While traditional conflicts between nation-states persist, new dynamics are emerging. Future regional conflicts may not conform to conventional warfare patterns. Non-state actors, insurgent groups, and cyber warfare capabilities have introduced new complexities into the realm of conflict.

Emergence of Non-State Actors: The emergence of non-state actors as significant players in regional conflicts represents a notable shift in the nature of warfare. These actors often operate with a degree of flexibility and adaptability that can challenge traditional state-centric military strategies. Understanding their motivations, funding sources, and strategies is essential. It involves exploring the complex web of political, social, and economic factors that contribute to their rise and impact on regional stability. Moreover, analyzing their connections across borders and assessing their capacity to disrupt established state structures is vital for predicting the trajectory of future conflicts.

Asymmetrical Warfare: Asymmetrical warfare introduces a level of unpredictability and innovation into conflicts. When parties with varying levels of military power engage, tactics can range from guerrilla warfare to cyberattacks. Examining asymmetrical warfare involves delving into the strategies employed by weaker actors to offset their disadvantages. This examination encompasses the study of insurgent tactics, the use of unconventional weapons, and the vulnerabilities of more technologically advanced adversaries. An in-depth analysis of asymmetrical warfare allows for a better understanding of how conflicts evolve and how states can adapt their defense strategies.

Insurgent Movements: The resurgence of insurgent movements in different regions requires a nuanced examination. These movements often arise due to grievances related to governance, social inequality, or ethnic tensions. Exploring insurgent movements involves analyzing their objectives, recruitment strategies, and external support networks. Understanding their motivations and the factors that enable their survival and growth is crucial. Additionally, examining the dynamics of negotiations and peace processes with insurgent groups can shed light on potential pathways to conflict resolution.

Cyber Warfare and Information Warfare: Cyber warfare and information warfare represent a growing challenge in modern conflicts. These forms of conflict extend beyond physical battlefields into the digital realm. Analyzing cyber warfare involves examining the capabilities and tactics used by state and non-state actors to infiltrate computer systems, disrupt critical infrastructure, and steal sensitive information. Information warfare explores the spread of disinformation, propaganda, and attempts to manipulate public opinion. It also involves assessing the vulnerabilities of societies and institutions to these tactics and devising strategies to counter them effectively.

Globalization and Interconnectedness: Globalization has interconnected regions in unprecedented ways, influencing the dynamics of regional conflicts. Understanding the geopolitical dimensions of globalization is vital. It involves exploring how economic interdependencies, trade networks, and alliances can both contribute to regional stability and exacerbate conflicts. Additionally, analyzing how international organizations and diplomatic efforts influence regional conflicts is crucial. This examination helps policymakers anticipate potential conflicts and work towards peaceful resolutions.

Resource Scarcity and Environmental Factors: Resource scarcity, exacerbated by environmental changes like climate change, can serve as a catalyst for conflicts. Examining the intersection of resource scarcity and conflict involves analyzing the competition for essential resources such as water, arable land, and minerals. It also encompasses exploring how environmental factors, like rising sea levels or extreme weather events, can exacerbate existing tensions. Understanding the complex relationship between resource scarcity, environmental stressors, and conflict dynamics is essential for devising strategies to prevent resource-driven conflicts.

Humanitarian Consequences: An analysis of conflicts would be incomplete without considering their humanitarian impact. Large-scale conflicts often result in displacement, loss of life, and profound suffering. Examining the humanitarian consequences involves assessing the needs of affected populations, the challenges of delivering aid in conflict zones, and the long-term recovery and reconciliation efforts required. Additionally, it involves exploring how international humanitarian organizations and relief efforts operate in conflict environments. Analyzing the humanitarian dimension underscores the urgency of conflict prevention and resolution.

In summary, each aspect of the shifting landscape of conflict is a complex and interconnected component. By analyzing these elements individually and collectively, we can gain a comprehensive understanding of the multifaceted nature of regional conflicts. Such understanding is essential for policymakers, diplomats, and scholars seeking to address and mitigate the challenges posed by future conflicts.

Resource Scarcity and Competition:

One driving factor behind future regional conflicts is the competition for scarce resources. As the global population continues to grow, demand for essential resources such as water, energy, and arable land intensifies. Regions that are already grappling with resource scarcity may become flashpoints for conflict. Understanding the intricate links between resource availability, climate change, and geopolitical tensions is vital for assessing the likelihood of future conflicts.

Resource scarcity and competition are central factors in the potential for future regional conflicts. The interaction between these elements and geopolitical dynamics is complex and requires in-depth examination.

1. **Water Scarcity:** Water scarcity is a critical issue, and it often intersects with political boundaries. Regions dependent on shared water resources, such as river basins, can become hotspots for conflict. Analyzing water scarcity involves studying the allocation of water resources, the impact of climate change on water availability, and the role of international water treaties. Understanding the historical and ongoing disputes over water rights is essential for anticipating future conflicts.

2. **Energy Resources:** The competition for energy resources, including fossil fuels and renewable energy, is a driving force in geopolitics. Future conflicts may arise from struggles over access to energy sources, energy infrastructure, or control of key energy transit routes. Energy resource competition involves assessing the role of energy as both a driver of conflicts and a potential catalyst for cooperation through energy diplomacy.

3. **Arable Land and Food Security:** Ensuring food security is a fundamental challenge for growing populations. The competition for arable land and resources required for agriculture can lead to conflicts over territory and resources. Examining this aspect involves analyzing how climate change impacts agricultural productivity, the role of land tenure systems, and the potential for conflicts related to food production and distribution.

4. **Minerals and Rare Earth Elements:** Rare earth elements and minerals are essential for various industries, including technology and defense. Regions with significant reserves of these resources may become focal points for competition. Understanding the global supply chains, the geopolitical significance of resource-rich areas, and the potential for conflicts related to resource extraction and trade is crucial.

5. **Climate Change and Resource Security:** Climate change exacerbates resource scarcity by altering weather patterns, sea levels, and ecosystems. Analyzing the impact of climate change on resource availability, including the potential for climate-induced migration and displacement, is essential. Additionally, exploring international efforts to address climate-related resource challenges, such as the Paris Agreement, provides insights into global responses to this complex issue.

6. **Geopolitical Strategies:** Nations employ various strategies to secure access to critical resources. This includes diplomatic negotiations, trade agreements, and, in some cases, military posturing. Examining the geopolitical strategies employed by nations to secure resource access and the potential for resource-driven conflicts provides insights into the role of resource scarcity in shaping global politics.

7. **Conflict Resolution and Resource Management:** Understanding how conflicts related to resource scarcity can be managed and resolved is vital for preventing escalation. Examining successful cases of resource conflict resolution, as well as the role of international organizations in mediating disputes, can inform strategies for maintaining peace in resource-scarce regions.

In summary, resource scarcity and competition are multifaceted drivers of future regional conflicts. Their intersection with geopolitical interests, climate change, and international relations creates complex challenges. By comprehensively analyzing these elements, policymakers and analysts can develop strategies to address the root causes of resource-driven conflicts and work towards peaceful and sustainable solutions.

Geopolitical Rivalries:

Geopolitical rivalries among nations can spark regional conflicts. The pursuit of strategic interests, territorial disputes, and influence in key regions can lead to tensions that escalate into full-scale conflicts. An analysis of historical and contemporary geopolitical rivalries provides insights into potential conflict zones and their underlying causes.

Geopolitical rivalries are significant drivers of potential future regional conflicts. These rivalries can be influenced by a range of factors, including strategic interests, territorial disputes, and the quest for influence in key regions. Analyzing both historical and contemporary geopolitical rivalries provides valuable insights into potential conflict zones and the root causes of these tensions.

1. **Territorial Disputes:** Territorial disputes over land and maritime boundaries are common sources of geopolitical rivalries. Examining historical conflicts and ongoing disputes, such as those in the South China Sea, the India-Pakistan border, or territorial claims in the Arctic, helps understand how unresolved territorial issues can fuel regional tensions. Additionally, the role of international law and dispute resolution mechanisms in addressing territorial disputes is essential to consider.

2. **Strategic Interests:** Nations often pursue strategic interests related to security, access to resources, or geopolitical influence. Analyzing the strategic interests of major powers in specific regions, such as the Middle East, the South Caucasus, or the Indo-Pacific, sheds light on potential areas of conflict. This includes assessing the role of military alliances and defense posturing in reinforcing strategic interests.

3. **Regional Power Dynamics:** Geopolitical rivalries can emerge from shifts in regional power dynamics. Studying the rise of regional powers and their interactions with established global powers provides insights into the complex web of alliances and rivalries. The influence of regional organizations, such as the European Union, the African Union, or ASEAN, in shaping regional dynamics is also a crucial aspect.

4. **Resource Access:** Access to critical resources, including energy, minerals, and waterways, can drive geopolitical competition. Analyzing how nations vie for control or access to these resources in regions like the South China Sea, the Persian Gulf, or the Arctic Ocean reveals the role of resource geopolitics in shaping conflicts.

5. **Influence in Key Regions:** Nations may seek to expand their influence in strategically important regions. Understanding the motives behind efforts to gain influence, whether through diplomatic means, economic partnerships, or military presence, is essential. The role of regional power brokers and non-state actors in influencing geopolitical rivalries should also be considered.

6. **Historical Precedents:** Historical examples of geopolitical rivalries that escalated into conflicts offer valuable lessons. Analyzing past conflicts, such as the Cold War rivalry between the United States and the Soviet Union or regional conflicts in

the Balkans, helps identify patterns and triggers for conflict escalation.

7. **Diplomatic Efforts:** Diplomacy plays a critical role in managing geopolitical rivalries and preventing conflicts. Examining diplomatic initiatives, negotiations, and conflict resolution mechanisms can provide insights into the potential for peaceful resolution of disputes and the role of international organizations, such as the United Nations, in mediating rivalries.

In summary, geopolitical rivalries are complex and multifaceted, with implications for regional stability and global security. Understanding the historical context, strategic interests, and evolving power dynamics within regions prone to rivalries is essential for predicting and addressing potential future conflicts. Additionally, exploring diplomatic avenues for conflict resolution is vital for promoting peace and stability in regions marked by geopolitical tensions.

Proxy Wars and Multilateral Dynamics:

Future regional conflicts may also involve proxy wars, where external powers support opposing factions within a region. Multilateral dynamics, including the roles of international organizations and alliances, can either exacerbate or mitigate regional tensions. Understanding the complexities of proxy conflicts and the potential for international intervention is crucial for assessing the trajectory of regional conflicts.

The specter of future regional conflicts raises the possibility of proxy wars, where external powers provide support to opposing factions within a region. Multilateral dynamics, including the roles of international organizations and alliances, play a critical role in shaping these conflicts. Analyzing the complexities of proxy wars and the potential for international intervention is essential for understanding the trajectory of regional conflicts.

1. **Proxy War Dynamics:** Proxy wars involve external actors providing military, financial, or logistical support to opposing groups within a region. These external actors may pursue their strategic interests, ideological goals, or seek to influence the outcome of a regional conflict. Examining historical examples, such as the proxy wars during the Cold War or more recent conflicts in Syria and Yemen, reveals patterns of external involvement and its impact on regional stability.

2. **Motives of External Powers:** Understanding the motives of external powers for intervening in regional conflicts is crucial. Motives can range from securing access to resources and markets to countering rival powers or ideological alignment. Analyzing the objectives and interests of key external actors, including major powers and

regional players, sheds light on the drivers of proxy conflicts.

3. **Regional Power Struggles:** Proxy conflicts often reflect broader regional power struggles. These struggles may involve competition for influence, control of strategic territories, or disputes over regional leadership. Studying regional dynamics, alliances, and power balances in regions like the Middle East, Eastern Europe, or the Indo-Pacific helps assess the potential for proxy wars.

4. **Impact on Regional Stability:** Proxy wars can have profound consequences for regional stability, often exacerbating conflict and humanitarian crises. Examining the impact of proxy conflicts on local populations, displacement, and the overall security situation is essential. It also highlights the role of regional organizations, such as the Arab League or the African Union, in mediating or exacerbating regional tensions.

5. **International Organizations:** International organizations, such as the United Nations and its specialized agencies, play a role in conflict prevention and resolution. Analyzing the effectiveness of international organizations in mediating regional conflicts and the role of peacekeeping missions is crucial. It also involves assessing the challenges and limitations faced by

these organizations in maintaining peace and security.

6. **Alliances and Coalitions:** Alliances and coalitions among states can shape the course of regional conflicts. Examining the role of military alliances like NATO, regional security arrangements, and ad-hoc coalitions in regional conflicts provides insights into the dynamics of collective security and deterrence.

7. **Conflict Resolution Efforts:** The potential for international intervention in proxy wars raises questions about conflict resolution efforts. Analyzing diplomatic initiatives, ceasefire agreements, and peace negotiations involving external actors is essential for assessing prospects for conflict de-escalation and resolution.

8. **Humanitarian Implications:** Proxy conflicts often have severe humanitarian implications, including civilian casualties, displacement, and food insecurity. Understanding the humanitarian consequences and the role of humanitarian organizations in providing aid and protection to affected populations is vital.

In summary, the dynamics of proxy wars and multilateral interventions in regional conflicts are multifaceted and can significantly impact regional stability and global security. Examining the motives of external powers, regional power struggles, and the effectiveness of international organizations and alliances provides a comprehensive understanding of the complexities involved in proxy conflicts. Additionally, assessing the humanitarian implications underscores the urgency of addressing these conflicts and seeking peaceful resolutions.

Cyber Warfare and Hybrid Threats:

The digital age has introduced new dimensions to conflict, including cyber warfare and hybrid threats. Future conflicts may involve cyberattacks on critical infrastructure, disinformation campaigns, and other unconventional tactics. Analyzing the capabilities and vulnerabilities in the realm of cyber warfare is essential for anticipating potential threats and understanding their impact on regional stability.

1. **Cyber Warfare Strategies:** Cyber warfare encompasses a wide range of strategies aimed at disrupting or compromising digital systems and networks. These strategies may include offensive tactics like malware deployment, denial-of-service attacks, and espionage. A thorough analysis of cyber warfare strategies reveals the methods employed by both state and non-state actors in future conflicts.

2. **Critical Infrastructure Vulnerabilities:** Critical infrastructure, such as power grids,

transportation systems, and communication networks, is highly susceptible to cyberattacks. Exploring the vulnerabilities of critical infrastructure is essential to grasp the potential consequences of successful cyberattacks, which can disrupt essential services and impact regional stability.

3. **State and Non-State Actors:** Cyber warfare is not limited to nation-states. Non-state actors, including hacktivist groups and cybercriminal organizations, can also engage in cyber aggression. Examining the capabilities, motivations, and actions of these actors provides valuable insights into the evolving threat landscape.

4. **Information Warfare and Disinformation:** Hybrid threats often involve information warfare and disinformation campaigns aimed at manipulating public perception and creating confusion. Investigating the use of fake news, propaganda, and social media manipulation during conflicts sheds light on the tactics employed to shape narratives and influence behavior.

5. **Attribution and Accountability:** One of the significant challenges in cyber warfare is attributing cyberattacks to specific actors. Understanding methods for attributing cyberattacks, along with international norms and

mechanisms for accountability, contributes to the assessment of how nations respond to cyber threats.

6. **Response and Defense Strategies**: Preparedness for cyber threats necessitates the development of response and defense strategies. These strategies include cybersecurity measures, incident response plans, and international cooperation in countering cyber threats. Analyzing these measures offers insights into regional stability and security.

7. **Regulatory Frameworks**: Cyber warfare operates within legal and ethical frameworks that are continually evolving. Examining national and international regulatory frameworks for cyber warfare and cybercrime helps understand the legal and ethical considerations involved in actions and responses during conflicts.

8. **Hybrid Warfare Scenarios**: Hybrid threats frequently combine traditional and cyber tactics. Analyzing hypothetical scenarios of hybrid warfare in various regions allows for an assessment of the potential for such conflicts and their implications for regional stability.

9. **Deterrence and Norms**: Establishing effective deterrence mechanisms and international norms is an ongoing effort in the realm of cyber warfare. Investigating efforts to deter cyber aggression and

promote responsible state behavior in cyberspace contributes to the prevention of conflicts.

10. **Cybersecurity Capacity Building:** Capacity building in cybersecurity is vital, especially for countries with vulnerabilities. Studying initiatives aimed at enhancing the cybersecurity capabilities of nations in regions prone to conflicts is crucial for regional security.

In summary, cyber warfare and hybrid threats represent evolving challenges in the modern conflict landscape. Understanding the various strategies employed, vulnerabilities of critical infrastructure, attribution methods, response strategies, and regulatory frameworks is essential for assessing the potential impact of cyber warfare on regional stability. Additionally, analyzing scenarios involving hybrid threats helps anticipate and prepare for complex conflict scenarios in the digital age.

Conflict Resolution and Diplomacy:

While the discussion revolves around the possibility of future conflicts, it is equally important to explore avenues for conflict resolution and diplomacy. Diplomatic efforts, peace negotiations, and conflict prevention strategies play a pivotal role in mitigating the likelihood of large-scale regional conflicts.

Examining successful and unsuccessful diplomatic initiatives provides valuable insights into pathways for peaceful resolution.

While the discussion revolves around the possibility of future conflicts, it is equally important to explore avenues for conflict resolution and diplomacy. Diplomatic efforts, peace negotiations, and conflict prevention strategies play a pivotal role in mitigating the likelihood of large-scale regional conflicts. Examining successful and unsuccessful diplomatic initiatives provides valuable insights into pathways for peaceful resolution.

1. **Historical Diplomatic Successes:** A comprehensive analysis of historical diplomatic successes can shed light on effective conflict resolution strategies. Examples such as the Camp David Accords, which normalized relations between Egypt and Israel, or the Dayton Agreement that ended the Bosnian War, demonstrate the potential for diplomacy to bring about lasting peace.

2. **Failed Diplomatic Efforts:** Understanding the reasons behind failed diplomatic efforts is equally important. Examining instances where negotiations broke down, such as the Israeli-Palestinian conflict or the Syrian civil war, offers insights into the challenges and barriers to peace.

3. **Conflict Prevention Mechanisms:** Conflict prevention is a proactive approach to avoiding conflicts before they escalate. Exploring mechanisms like early warning systems, confidence-building measures, and preventive diplomacy allows for an assessment of their effectiveness in averting potential conflicts.

4. **Multilateral Diplomacy:** Multilateral diplomacy involves the collaboration of multiple nations and international organizations in conflict resolution efforts. Analyzing the roles of organizations like the United Nations, regional bodies, and peacekeeping missions in resolving regional conflicts helps evaluate the impact of multilateral approaches.

5. **Track II Diplomacy:** Track II diplomacy involves unofficial, non-governmental efforts to facilitate peace talks. Studying the contributions of non-governmental organizations, academic institutions, and civil society in conflict resolution provides insights into alternative diplomatic channels.

6. **Peacebuilding and Post-Conflict Reconstruction:** Peacebuilding initiatives aim to stabilize regions after conflicts have ceased. Examining post-conflict reconstruction efforts, including disarmament, demobilization, and reintegration (DDR) programs, helps assess their effectiveness in sustaining peace.

7. **Mediation and Third-Party Involvement:** The role of mediators and third-party actors in resolving conflicts is pivotal. Analyzing the impact of neutral mediators and the strategies they employ contributes to an understanding of successful mediation processes.

8. **Peace Treaties and Agreements:** The negotiation and implementation of peace treaties and agreements are crucial milestones in conflict resolution. Investigating the terms, compliance mechanisms, and long-term impacts of such agreements informs assessments of their efficacy.

9. **Diplomatic Failures and Impediments:** Diplomatic failures often result from complex geopolitical factors, power imbalances, and intractable issues. Delving into these impediments to successful diplomacy reveals the challenges that diplomats face in resolving conflicts.

10. **Lessons Learned and Best Practices:** Reflecting on lessons learned from past diplomatic experiences and identifying best practices in conflict resolution is vital. This knowledge can inform the development of future diplomatic strategies and enhance the chances of successful outcomes.

11. **Diplomatic Innovations:** Contemporary diplomacy is evolving with the introduction of innovative approaches, such as digital diplomacy and citizen diplomacy. Analyzing these innovations and their impact on conflict

resolution processes is crucial in adapting to changing diplomatic landscapes.

In conclusion, conflict resolution and diplomacy offer essential pathways to prevent and mitigate large-scale regional conflicts. By examining historical successes and failures, conflict prevention mechanisms, multilateral diplomacy, and the contributions of non-governmental actors, we gain valuable insights into how diplomacy can shape the future of international relations and regional stability.

Humanitarian Consequences:

Lastly, an exploration of future regional conflicts must address the humanitarian consequences. Large-scale conflicts result in displacement, loss of life, and profound suffering. Understanding the potential humanitarian toll and the strategies for mitigating these impacts underscores the urgency of conflict prevention and resolution.

Lastly, an exploration of future regional conflicts must address the humanitarian consequences. Large-scale conflicts result in displacement, loss of life, and profound suffering. Understanding the potential humanitarian toll and the strategies for mitigating these impacts underscores the urgency of conflict prevention and resolution.

1. **Displacement and Refugees:** Large-scale conflicts often lead to significant population displacement, both internally and across borders. Examining the causes and consequences of displacement, as well as the challenges faced by refugees and internally displaced persons, provides insights into the scale of the humanitarian crisis.

2. **Humanitarian Aid and Relief Efforts:** Humanitarian organizations play a critical role in providing aid and relief to conflict-affected populations. Analyzing the effectiveness of humanitarian interventions, including access to essential services, food, shelter, and medical care, helps assess their impact on mitigating suffering.

3. **Protection of Civilians:** Protecting civilians in conflict zones is a fundamental humanitarian principle. Investigating measures taken to safeguard the lives and well-being of non-combatants, including the role of peacekeepers and international humanitarian law, sheds light on the challenges and successes in upholding this principle.

4. **Healthcare and Medical Services:** Conflicts disrupt healthcare systems and access to medical services. Understanding the impact on healthcare infrastructure, disease outbreaks, and the provision of medical care in conflict zones is vital for addressing the health-related humanitarian consequences.

5. **Education and Child Protection:** Conflict disrupts education and poses risks to children's well-being. Examining the impact on education systems, child protection measures, and the long-term consequences for children affected by conflict highlights the importance of addressing these specific humanitarian concerns.

6. **Psychosocial Support and Trauma:** Conflict-related trauma and psychosocial challenges affect the mental health of individuals and communities. Assessing the availability of psychosocial support, trauma counseling, and mental health services in conflict-affected areas is crucial for understanding the human toll of conflicts.

7. **Gender-Based Violence:** Conflict zones often see an increase in gender-based violence. Analyzing the prevalence, causes, and responses to gender-based violence in conflict situations helps address the specific vulnerabilities faced by women and girls.

8. **Access to Food and Water:** Food and water security are essential humanitarian concerns during conflicts. Exploring issues related to food distribution, access to clean water, and efforts to prevent famine provides insights into the challenges of meeting basic needs in conflict-affected regions.

9. **Internally Displaced Persons (IDPs):** Understanding the experiences and needs of internally displaced persons, who remain within their own countries but are forced to flee their homes, is critical for addressing their unique vulnerabilities and ensuring their protection.

10. **International Humanitarian Law:** The role of international humanitarian law in protecting civilians and regulating the conduct of armed conflict is significant. Examining the implementation and enforcement of these legal frameworks contributes to understanding the legal aspects of humanitarian protection.

11. **Humanitarian Coordination:** Effective humanitarian response often requires coordination among multiple actors, including governments, non-governmental organizations, and international agencies. Analyzing the coordination mechanisms and challenges in humanitarian efforts enhances the effectiveness of relief operations.

12. **Lessons Learned from Past Conflicts:** Learning from past conflicts and humanitarian responses is essential. Identifying lessons, best practices, and areas for improvement in humanitarian action informs strategies for addressing future humanitarian consequences of regional conflicts.

In conclusion, an in-depth examination of the humanitarian consequences of future regional conflicts is essential for both proactive conflict prevention and effective response. By understanding the impact on displaced populations, the role of humanitarian organizations, and the challenges in providing protection and essential services, we can better address the urgent needs of those affected by conflicts and strive for a more compassionate and coordinated humanitarian response.

By discussing the possibility of future regional conflicts within these contexts, we gain a deeper understanding of the complex factors at play. This understanding is instrumental in shaping policies, fostering diplomacy, and working towards a more peaceful and stable global future.

Chapter 12: Protecting Earth
International Efforts

Analyze the plans of world rulers, secret rulers, the UN, and its sub-sections to protect Earth.

United Nations' Sustainable Development Goals (SDGs):

The United Nations has adopted a set of 17 Sustainable Development Goals aimed at addressing global challenges, including environmental protection. Examining the progress and strategies related to environmental sustainability within the SDGs provides insights into international efforts to protect the Earth.

1. **Goal 1: No Poverty:** While Goal 1 primarily addresses poverty eradication, it indirectly contributes to environmental protection by reducing vulnerability to environmental shocks and disasters among impoverished populations.

2. **Goal 2: Zero Hunger:** Ensuring food security and sustainable agriculture (Goal 2) intersects with environmental sustainability through responsible land use, conservation practices, and efforts to reduce food waste.

3. **Goal 3: Good Health and Well-Being:** Promoting good health and well-being (Goal 3) includes addressing health impacts related to

environmental factors, such as air and water quality, and the prevention of diseases linked to environmental risks.

4. **Goal 6: Clean Water and Sanitation:** Goal 6 focuses on ensuring access to clean water and sanitation. It directly contributes to environmental protection by safeguarding freshwater sources and ecosystems.

5. **Goal 7: Affordable and Clean Energy:** Expanding access to affordable and clean energy (Goal 7) is essential for reducing reliance on fossil fuels and mitigating climate change.

6. **Goal 9: Industry, Innovation, and Infrastructure:** Goal 9 promotes sustainable industrialization and innovation, which includes eco-friendly technologies and infrastructure development that minimizes environmental impacts.

7. **Goal 11: Sustainable Cities and Communities:** Creating sustainable cities and communities (Goal 11) involves urban planning that considers environmental sustainability, including reduced emissions and improved public transportation.

8. **Goal 12: Responsible Consumption and Production:** Goal 12 emphasizes responsible consumption and production patterns, reducing resource waste and environmental harm.

9. **Goal 13: Climate Action:** Goal 13 specifically targets climate action. This goal calls for urgent measures to combat climate change and its impacts.

10. **Goal 14: Life Below Water:** Goal 14 focuses on conserving and sustainably using the oceans, seas, and marine resources.

11. **Goal 15: Life on Land:** Goal 15 emphasizes the protection, restoration, and sustainable management of terrestrial ecosystems, including forests, biodiversity, and land resources.

12. **Goal 17: Partnerships for the Goals:** Goal 17 highlights the importance of global partnerships for sustainable development, including environmental protection.

Examining the environmental aspects of these SDGs, along with their progress, strategies, challenges, and collaborations, provides a comprehensive view of international efforts to protect the Earth's environment and resources.

Climate Change Agreements:

International agreements such as the Paris Agreement play a pivotal role in addressing climate change. Analyzing the commitments of nations to reduce greenhouse gas emissions and limit global warming helps assess the effectiveness of global climate efforts.

International agreements such as the Paris Agreement play a pivotal role in addressing climate change. Analyzing the commitments of nations to reduce greenhouse gas emissions and limit global warming helps assess the effectiveness of global climate efforts.

1. **The Paris Agreement:** The Paris Agreement, adopted in 2015 under the United Nations Framework Convention on Climate Change (UNFCCC), is a landmark accord that brings nations together to combat climate change. Under this agreement, countries pledge to keep global warming well below 2 degrees Celsius above pre-industrial levels and aim for limiting it to 1.5 degrees Celsius.

2. **Nationally Determined Contributions (NDCs):** One of the key components of the Paris Agreement is the submission of Nationally Determined Contributions (NDCs) by each participating country. These documents outline each nation's specific climate action targets and strategies for reducing greenhouse gas emissions. Analyzing the adequacy and ambition of these NDCs is crucial for assessing the global commitment to combating climate change.

3. **Progress Monitoring:** Continuous monitoring and reporting of emissions and progress towards NDCs are essential aspects of the Paris Agreement. Evaluating the transparency and accuracy of these reports provides insights into whether countries are staying on track to achieve their climate goals.

4. **Climate Financing:** International climate agreements also address the financial aspects of climate action. The agreement recognizes the need for financial support to developing nations to help them adapt to climate change and transition to low-carbon economies. Assessing the adequacy and effectiveness of climate financing mechanisms is vital for equitable and effective climate mitigation and adaptation.

5. **Global Cooperation:** Climate change is a global challenge that requires cooperation among nations. Analyzing the level of cooperation, information sharing, and technology transfer among countries helps assess the collaborative efforts to address climate change.

6. **Challenges and Barriers:** While international climate agreements are critical, they also face challenges and barriers. These can include issues related to enforcement, the role of non-state actors, and geopolitical tensions. Examining these challenges provides insights into areas that require improvement to enhance the effectiveness of climate agreements.

7. **Adaptation and Resilience:** In addition to mitigation efforts, climate agreements also address adaptation and building resilience to the impacts of climate change. Assessing the strategies and actions countries are taking to adapt to changing climate conditions is essential for understanding their commitment to protecting vulnerable communities and ecosystems.

8. **Innovation and Technology Transfer:** Technological advancements and innovation play a significant role in addressing climate change. Evaluating the transfer of green technologies and the development of clean energy solutions can highlight areas of progress and opportunities for further innovation.

9. **Civil Society and Public Engagement:** Climate agreements often involve civil society participation and public engagement. Analyzing the involvement and advocacy of non-governmental organizations and the general public can shed light on the societal commitment to addressing climate change.

By examining these aspects of international climate change agreements, we can gain a comprehensive understanding of the global effort to combat climate change, identify areas of progress, and pinpoint challenges that require attention. This analysis is crucial for assessing the effectiveness of these agreements in protecting the environment and mitigating the impacts of climate change.

Biodiversity Conservation Conventions:

Conventions like the Convention on Biological Diversity focus on conserving biodiversity worldwide. Investigating the implementation and outcomes of such agreements sheds light on international endeavors to protect Earth's ecosystems and species.

1. **Convention on Biological Diversity (CBD):** The CBD, adopted in 1992, is a significant international treaty aimed at conserving biodiversity, promoting sustainable use of biological resources, and ensuring the fair and equitable sharing of benefits arising from genetic resources. Examining the progress made in achieving the CBD's objectives, including the Aichi Biodiversity Targets and the post-2020 Global Biodiversity Framework, provides insights into global efforts to protect biodiversity.

2. **National Biodiversity Strategies and Action Plans (NBSAPs):** Under the CBD, countries are encouraged to develop National Biodiversity Strategies and Action Plans (NBSAPs) to guide

their biodiversity conservation efforts. Analyzing the development, implementation, and effectiveness of NBSAPs offers a view of each country's commitment to preserving its unique biodiversity.

3. **Protected Areas and Conservation Initiatives:** Many international biodiversity conventions emphasize the establishment and management of protected areas to safeguard critical habitats and species. Assessing the expansion of protected areas, their management, and their contribution to biodiversity conservation provides insights into global conservation efforts.

4. **Threatened Species Conservation:** International conventions often address the conservation of threatened and endangered species. Examining the progress in protecting and recovering these species, as well as the enforcement of regulations against illegal wildlife trade, offers insights into international endeavors to prevent species extinction.

5. **Sustainable Use of Biological Resources:** Sustainable utilization of biological resources is a key aspect of biodiversity conservation. Analyzing the implementation of sustainable practices in agriculture, fisheries, forestry, and other sectors helps assess the global commitment to balancing human needs with ecological conservation.

6. **Ecosystem Restoration:** Ecosystem restoration is increasingly recognized as a vital component of biodiversity conservation. Investigating global initiatives for restoring degraded ecosystems, such as reforestation and wetland restoration, provides insights into efforts to reverse habitat loss and biodiversity decline.

7. **Indigenous and Local Community Involvement:** Biodiversity conservation conventions often stress the importance of involving indigenous and local communities in conservation efforts. Examining the role and participation of these communities in conservation initiatives helps evaluate the inclusivity of international conservation agreements.

8. **Global Biodiversity Targets:** Similar to climate agreements, biodiversity conventions set specific targets and goals. Analyzing progress toward achieving these targets, including the reduction of biodiversity loss and the restoration of ecosystems, highlights the effectiveness of international biodiversity conservation efforts.

9. **Challenges and Obstacles:** While international biodiversity conventions are critical, they face challenges such as insufficient funding, habitat fragmentation, and the impact of climate change. Investigating these challenges provides insights into areas that require attention and improvement in global biodiversity conservation.

10. **Multilateral Cooperation:** Biodiversity conservation often requires multilateral cooperation, especially for transboundary conservation areas. Evaluating the level of cooperation, data sharing, and collaborative research among countries helps assess the effectiveness of international biodiversity conventions.

By examining these aspects of international biodiversity conservation conventions, we can gain a comprehensive understanding of global efforts to protect Earth's ecosystems and species. This analysis helps identify progress, challenges, and opportunities for enhanced conservation measures on a global scale.

International Environmental Organizations:

Numerous international organizations, both within and outside the UN system, work on environmental protection. Examining the roles and actions of organizations like the United Nations Environment Programme (UNEP) and the World Wildlife Fund (WWF) contributes to understanding global environmental initiatives.

1. **United Nations Environment Programme (UNEP):** UNEP is a leading global environmental authority that plays a crucial role in coordinating international efforts to address environmental

challenges. Analyzing UNEP's programs and initiatives, including its work on climate change, biodiversity conservation, and pollution control, provides insights into the UN's contributions to global environmental protection.

2. **World Wildlife Fund (WWF):** WWF is one of the world's largest and most influential conservation organizations. Examining WWF's projects, campaigns, and collaborations with governments and local communities offers insights into how non-governmental organizations (NGOs) contribute to global environmental conservation efforts.

3. **Environmental Research and Advocacy:** International environmental organizations often conduct research and advocacy to raise awareness about pressing environmental issues. Investigating their research findings, policy recommendations, and public engagement activities helps gauge their influence on global environmental agendas.

4. **Wildlife Conservation:** Many international organizations focus on wildlife conservation, particularly for endangered species. Analyzing the impact of wildlife protection efforts, such as anti-poaching initiatives and habitat restoration projects, provides insights into the global commitment to safeguarding biodiversity.

5. **Climate Change Mitigation and Adaptation:** Climate change is a top global environmental concern. Examining international organizations' contributions to climate change mitigation and adaptation efforts, including the promotion of renewable energy and climate resilience initiatives, helps assess progress in addressing this critical issue.

6. **Collaboration and Partnerships:** International environmental organizations often collaborate with governments, businesses, and other NGOs. Evaluating the nature and effectiveness of these partnerships in achieving environmental goals highlights the importance of multi-stakeholder cooperation.

7. **Advocacy for Sustainable Practices:** Many organizations advocate for sustainable practices in various sectors, from agriculture and forestry to fisheries and energy. Investigating their efforts to promote sustainable production and consumption patterns contributes to understanding global sustainability initiatives.

8. **Environmental Education and Outreach:** Environmental organizations engage in educational activities to raise awareness and promote responsible environmental behavior. Analyzing their educational programs and outreach campaigns helps assess their role in fostering environmental stewardship.

9. **Policy Influence:** International environmental organizations often engage in policy advocacy and contribute to the development of international agreements and regulations. Assessing their influence on global environmental policy-making sheds light on their impact on the legal framework for environmental protection.

10. **Challenges and Achievements:** While international environmental organizations have made significant contributions, they also face challenges such as funding constraints and political resistance. Evaluating their achievements and the obstacles they encounter provides a balanced view of their effectiveness in addressing global environmental issues.

By examining these aspects of international environmental organizations, we can gain a comprehensive understanding of their roles in global environmental protection and sustainability efforts. This analysis helps identify areas of success, challenges, and opportunities for strengthening global environmental initiatives.

Scientific Collaboration:

International scientific collaborations are essential for understanding and addressing environmental challenges. Analyzing research initiatives, data-sharing efforts, and scientific assessments helps gauge the role of scientific communities in Earth protection.

1. **Global Research Initiatives:** Scientific collaboration spans across borders and disciplines to tackle complex environmental issues. Examining global research initiatives, such as those related to climate science, biodiversity monitoring, and ecosystem health, highlights the collective efforts of scientists worldwide to advance environmental knowledge.

2. **Data Sharing and Open Science:** Effective environmental protection relies on accurate and up-to-date data. Investigating international efforts to share environmental data, promote open science practices, and develop standardized datasets underscores the importance of data accessibility for informed decision-making.

3. **Cross-Disciplinary Approaches:** Many environmental challenges require cross-disciplinary expertise. Analyzing how scientists from various fields, including ecology, climatology, geology, and social sciences, collaborate to address multifaceted issues like climate change adaptation and ecosystem restoration demonstrates the value of interdisciplinary research.

4. **Scientific Assessments:** International scientific assessments, such as those conducted by the Intergovernmental Panel on Climate Change

(IPCC) and the Intergovernmental Science-Policy Platform on Biodiversity and Ecosystem Services (IPBES), provide critical insights into the state of the environment. Assessing the impact of these assessments on policy decisions and public awareness highlights their role in shaping environmental protection strategies.

5. **Emerging Technologies:** Scientific collaboration often drives the development and application of emerging technologies for environmental monitoring and conservation. Exploring innovations in fields like remote sensing, environmental genomics, and artificial intelligence helps assess the potential for technological advancements to support Earth protection.

6. **Capacity Building:** Collaborative efforts extend to capacity building in developing regions. Evaluating initiatives that support scientific training, technology transfer, and knowledge exchange between countries sheds light on efforts to enhance global environmental expertise and equity.

7. **Policy-Relevant Research:** Many international scientific collaborations aim to produce policy-relevant research. Examining the impact of scientific findings on environmental policy formulation and implementation helps assess the

effectiveness of scientific contributions to Earth protection.

8. **Challenges and Funding:** Scientific collaboration faces challenges such as funding constraints and political interference. Analyzing the barriers to international research cooperation and the role of funding agencies in supporting environmental science provides insights into potential obstacles to progress.

9. **Communication and Outreach:** Effective communication of scientific findings is crucial for public awareness and policy adoption. Investigating how scientific communities engage in outreach, science communication, and public education activities contributes to understanding their role in shaping environmental attitudes and behaviors.

10. **Long-Term Monitoring:** Some scientific collaborations focus on long-term environmental monitoring efforts. Assessing the continuity and impact of monitoring programs, such as those tracking changes in ocean health or air quality, helps evaluate the effectiveness of sustained scientific observation.

By examining these aspects of scientific collaboration, we can gain a comprehensive view of how scientists worldwide contribute to the understanding and protection of Earth's environment. This analysis helps identify areas of success, challenges, and opportunities for strengthening global scientific efforts in environmental conservation and sustainability.

Human Rights and Environmental Justice:

The intersection of human rights and environmental protection is crucial. Examining international efforts to promote environmental justice, including the rights of vulnerable populations affected by environmental degradation, underscores the ethical dimension of Earth protection.

1. **Environmental Impact on Human Rights:** Investigating how environmental degradation, including pollution, habitat loss, and climate change, impacts the enjoyment of human rights is essential. This includes examining the rights to life, health, clean water, clean air, and a healthy environment, as recognized in international human rights agreements.

2. **Environmental Displacement and Migration:** Climate change and environmental disasters can lead to displacement and migration. Analyzing international efforts to address the rights of environmental migrants and internally displaced persons, as well as their access to protection and assistance, provides insights into responses to environmental displacement.

3. **Indigenous and Local Communities:** Indigenous and local communities often bear the brunt of environmental degradation. Examining initiatives that recognize and protect the rights of these communities, including land rights and the preservation of traditional knowledge, sheds light on efforts to address environmental justice.

4. **Environmental Impact Assessments:** Many international agreements and conventions require environmental impact assessments for development projects. Evaluating the effectiveness of such assessments in considering human rights impacts and engaging affected communities in decision-making processes is crucial for assessing environmental justice efforts.

5. **Environmental Defenders:** Environmental defenders, including activists and indigenous leaders, often face threats and violence. Analyzing international mechanisms and initiatives aimed at protecting environmental defenders and ensuring their rights to advocate for environmental protection contributes to understanding the challenges they encounter.

6. **Access to Environmental Information and Participation:** Environmental justice is facilitated by access to information and participation in environmental decision-making. Examining international efforts to promote transparency, public access to environmental information, and

the inclusion of marginalized groups in environmental governance helps assess progress in this area.

7. **Environmental Treaties and Protocols:** Many international environmental agreements address the rights of affected communities. Assessing the implementation and impact of such treaties, including the Aarhus Convention on access to information, public participation, and access to justice in environmental matters, provides insights into legal frameworks for environmental justice.

8. **Legal Redress and Remedies:** Analyzing mechanisms for legal redress and remedies for individuals and communities affected by environmental harm is essential. This includes examining access to national and international courts, as well as the role of human rights bodies in addressing environmental-related complaints.

9. **Corporate Accountability:** Environmental justice extends to corporate responsibility for environmental impacts. Investigating efforts to hold corporations accountable for environmental harm and human rights violations related to their activities contributes to understanding the role of business in Earth protection.

10. **Equity in Environmental Policies:** Environmental policies and initiatives should prioritize equity and justice. Assessing the

inclusivity and fairness of policies, including their distributional impacts on vulnerable populations, helps ensure that environmental protection efforts align with principles of justice.

By examining these aspects of the intersection between human rights and environmental protection, we gain a comprehensive understanding of international efforts to promote environmental justice. This analysis helps identify areas of progress, challenges, and opportunities for strengthening the ethical dimensions of Earth protection and ensuring the rights of all individuals and communities are respected in environmental decision-making and actions.

Space Exploration and Earth Observation:

Space agencies worldwide contribute to monitoring Earth's environment. Exploring the role of space exploration, satellite technology, and Earth observation in environmental monitoring and disaster management provides valuable insights.

1. **Remote Sensing and Environmental Monitoring:** Satellites equipped with remote sensing instruments play a crucial role in monitoring Earth's vital signs. They provide real-time data on a wide range of environmental parameters, including climate patterns, land cover changes,

deforestation, and sea level rise. Examining the capabilities of remote sensing technology helps assess its contribution to environmental protection.

2. **Climate Change Research:** Space-based observatories contribute significantly to climate change research. By tracking greenhouse gas concentrations, sea surface temperatures, and glacial melt rates from space, scientists can better understand climate trends and impacts. Analyzing international collaborations in climate monitoring through satellites sheds light on global efforts to address climate change.

3. **Natural Disaster Detection and Response:** Earth observation satellites are essential for early detection and response to natural disasters such as hurricanes, earthquakes, and wildfires. Investigating the coordination among space agencies and international organizations in disaster management provides insights into global preparedness and response mechanisms.

4. **Environmental Data Sharing:** International cooperation in sharing environmental data gathered from space is critical. Analyzing data-sharing agreements, protocols, and initiatives among nations helps assess the accessibility of crucial information for environmental protection and disaster mitigation.

5. **Monitoring Biodiversity and Ecosystems:** Satellites also contribute to monitoring biodiversity and ecosystems. They help track changes in habitats, wildlife populations, and the health of ecosystems. Examining how space technology supports biodiversity conservation and informs ecosystem management strategies contributes to global conservation efforts.

6. **Deforestation and Illegal Logging Detection:** Spaceborne technology can detect deforestation and illegal logging activities in remote areas. Analyzing initiatives and partnerships aimed at combating deforestation, preserving tropical rainforests, and addressing illegal logging through satellite monitoring contributes to forest conservation efforts.

7. **Oceans and Marine Conservation:** Satellites provide critical data for monitoring oceans and marine ecosystems. They help track ocean currents, sea surface temperatures, and the movement of marine species. Investigating how space technology supports international efforts to protect marine biodiversity and combat issues such as coral reef bleaching and overfishing is essential.

8. **Disaster Risk Reduction:** Space technology plays a role in disaster risk reduction by providing early warning systems for tsunamis, floods, and other hazards. Examining the effectiveness of these

systems in reducing the impact of disasters on vulnerable communities informs disaster risk reduction strategies.

9. **Space Debris and Environmental Impact:** Space exploration also poses environmental challenges, including the proliferation of space debris. Analyzing international agreements and initiatives aimed at mitigating the environmental impact of space activities contributes to space sustainability and Earth protection.

10. **Future Space Exploration Goals:** Exploring the future goals of space agencies and their alignment with environmental protection objectives provides insights into the evolving role of space exploration in addressing global environmental challenges.

By examining these aspects of space exploration, satellite technology, and Earth observation, we gain a comprehensive understanding of the contributions of space agencies and the international community to environmental monitoring and disaster management. This analysis helps assess the effectiveness of space-based tools in Earth protection and informs strategies for leveraging space technology for a sustainable and resilient future.

Global Environmental Funds:

International funds dedicated to environmental protection, such as the Green Climate Fund, support projects aimed at mitigating climate change and conserving ecosystems. Analyzing the allocation and impact of such funds helps assess financial contributions to Earth protection.

1. **Green Climate Fund (GCF):** The Green Climate Fund is a significant global financial mechanism dedicated to addressing climate change. It provides funding to developing countries to support climate adaptation and mitigation projects. Examining the allocation of resources by the GCF sheds light on international efforts to combat climate change and reduce greenhouse gas emissions.

2. **Biodiversity Conservation Funds:** Various international funds focus on conserving biodiversity and ecosystems. These funds support initiatives related to protected areas, wildlife conservation, and sustainable land use. Analyzing the projects funded by these mechanisms contributes to understanding global efforts to protect Earth's natural heritage.

3. **Renewable Energy Investment:** Funds and initiatives aimed at promoting renewable energy sources, such as the Global Environment Facility (GEF), play a critical role in reducing carbon emissions. Investigating the impact of renewable

energy investments on global energy transitions helps assess their contribution to environmental protection.

4. **Sustainable Development Goals Financing:** The financing of Sustainable Development Goals (SDGs), including those related to environmental sustainability, involves various international funding mechanisms. Analyzing how these funds are mobilized and utilized for projects related to clean water, clean energy, and ecosystem conservation provides insights into efforts to protect the Earth while promoting human well-being.

5. **Capacity Building and Technical Assistance:** In addition to financial support, global environmental funds often provide capacity-building and technical assistance to recipient countries. Examining the effectiveness of capacity-building programs in enhancing local expertise and institutional capacity for environmental management is essential.

6. **Monitoring and Evaluation:** International funds typically have rigorous monitoring and evaluation mechanisms to assess the impact of funded projects. Analyzing the evaluation reports and outcomes of funded initiatives helps determine the effectiveness of financial contributions to Earth protection.

7. **Adaptation and Resilience Projects:** Funds like the Adaptation Fund focus on supporting projects that enhance the resilience of communities and ecosystems to the impacts of climate change. Investigating the implementation and outcomes of adaptation projects provides insights into strategies for coping with environmental challenges.

8. **Transparency and Accountability:** Ensuring transparency and accountability in the allocation and utilization of global environmental funds is critical. Examining governance structures, reporting mechanisms, and accountability frameworks helps assess the integrity of these financial mechanisms.

9. **Private Sector Engagement:** Many global environmental funds engage with the private sector to mobilize additional resources for environmental projects. Analyzing the role of private sector partnerships and investments in supporting Earth protection initiatives contributes to a holistic understanding of funding sources.

10. **Challenges and Gaps:** It's essential to identify challenges and gaps in the allocation and utilization of global environmental funds. Understanding barriers to funding access, disparities in resource distribution, and potential

inefficiencies informs strategies for improving financial contributions to Earth protection.

By examining these aspects of global environmental funds, we gain insights into the financial mechanisms that support projects aimed at protecting Earth's environment. This analysis helps assess the effectiveness of international efforts to address environmental challenges and contributes to the broader goal of sustainable development and conservation.

Conflict Resolution and Environmental Diplomacy:

Conflicts often have environmental implications, and resolving conflicts can contribute to environmental protection. Examining diplomatic efforts to prevent or resolve conflicts with environmental consequences is essential.

1. **Resource-Based Conflicts:** Many conflicts are rooted in disputes over natural resources, such as water, land, and minerals. Environmental diplomacy involves mediating resource-based conflicts and finding sustainable solutions that safeguard both environmental integrity and human rights.

2. **Transboundary Environmental Issues:** Environmental challenges, such as pollution and ecosystem degradation, often cross national borders. Diplomatic efforts and agreements are necessary to address transboundary issues collaboratively. Analyzing successful negotiations and cooperative initiatives highlights the potential for diplomacy to mitigate environmental harm.

3. **Environmental Peacebuilding:** The concept of environmental peacebuilding recognizes that environmental issues can either exacerbate conflicts or provide opportunities for peacebuilding. Understanding how environmental factors, such as resource sharing agreements, can contribute to conflict resolution is crucial.

4. **Disaster Preparedness and Response:** Environmental diplomacy also plays a role in disaster preparedness and response. International cooperation in disaster management, including responses to natural disasters exacerbated by conflicts, contributes to the protection of vulnerable populations and ecosystems.

5. **Conservation Agreements in Conflict Zones:** In regions affected by armed conflicts, conserving biodiversity and protecting natural resources can be challenging. Analyzing efforts to negotiate conservation agreements and establish protected

areas in conflict zones demonstrates the potential for diplomacy to preserve critical ecosystems.

6. **International Conventions and Treaties**: Many international conventions and treaties address environmental issues with cross-border implications. Examining the role of diplomacy in the negotiation and enforcement of these agreements, such as the Convention on the Law of the Non-Navigational Uses of International Watercourses, provides insights into international efforts to protect shared resources.

7. **Conflict Prevention**: Diplomatic efforts are not limited to resolving ongoing conflicts; they also include conflict prevention. Identifying early warning signs of potential conflicts with environmental dimensions and taking proactive diplomatic measures can prevent the escalation of disputes.

8. **Post-Conflict Environmental Recovery**: After conflicts, environmental damage often requires post-conflict recovery and restoration efforts. Environmental diplomacy can facilitate cooperation in rehabilitating ecosystems and addressing long-term environmental consequences.

9. **Humanitarian and Environmental Aid**: Diplomatic negotiations are essential for ensuring the safe delivery of humanitarian and environmental aid to conflict-affected regions.

Analyzing the coordination of aid efforts helps understand the role of diplomacy in humanitarian and environmental assistance.

10. **Cross-Sectoral Collaboration:** Environmental diplomacy often involves collaboration between environmental organizations, humanitarian agencies, governments, and international bodies. Examining the effectiveness of cross-sectoral cooperation in addressing conflicts with environmental implications reveals opportunities for integrated approaches.

11. **Success Stories and Challenges:** Identifying success stories in conflict resolution and environmental diplomacy provides valuable lessons for future efforts. Additionally, recognizing the challenges and limitations of diplomatic interventions highlights areas where improvements are needed.

12. **Environmental Security:** Diplomacy also plays a role in addressing environmental security concerns, where environmental degradation can lead to conflicts. Analyzing diplomatic initiatives aimed at ensuring environmental security contributes to global stability.

By examining these aspects of conflict resolution and environmental diplomacy, we gain insights into the ways in which diplomatic efforts can contribute to both conflict prevention and environmental protection. This analysis helps assess the effectiveness of international endeavors to address conflicts with environmental consequences and underscores the interconnectedness of peace and environmental sustainability.

Global Agendas for Sustainability:

International forums and summits, such as the Earth Summit and the World Summit on Sustainable Development, set global agendas for sustainability. Analyzing the outcomes and commitments from these gatherings offers insights into the priorities of world leaders in protecting Earth.

1. **Agenda-Setting and Goal Formulation:** International forums provide platforms for leaders, policymakers, and experts to come together and set global sustainability agendas. These agendas often include defining specific goals, targets, and action plans to address environmental and sustainability challenges. Analyzing the formulation of these agendas reveals the consensus and divergences among nations.

2. **Sustainable Development Goals (SDGs):** The Earth Summit in 1992 laid the groundwork for the adoption of the Sustainable Development Goals (SDGs) by the United Nations. Examining the process of developing and adopting the SDGs, as

well as the progress toward their implementation, provides insights into the commitment of nations to a more sustainable future.

3. **Climate Agreements:** International climate agreements, such as the Paris Agreement, are often the outcomes of these global forums. Analyzing the negotiations, commitments, and progress toward climate goals underscores the importance of these agreements in mitigating climate change.

4. **Biodiversity Conservation:** Global forums also address biodiversity conservation. Agreements like the Convention on Biological Diversity (CBD) are discussed and refined in these settings. Evaluating the implementation of biodiversity conservation commitments highlights international efforts to protect Earth's ecosystems and species.

5. **Natural Resource Management:** Sustainable management of natural resources is a key aspect of global sustainability agendas. Forums often address issues related to responsible resource extraction, habitat protection, and equitable resource distribution. Examining progress in resource management goals reveals the challenges and successes in this area.

6. **Environmental Justice:** The concept of environmental justice, which addresses the equitable distribution of environmental benefits

and burdens, is increasingly integrated into global sustainability discussions. Analyzing discussions on environmental justice sheds light on efforts to ensure fairness in environmental decision-making.

7. **Civil Society and Stakeholder Involvement:** Global forums provide opportunities for civil society organizations, indigenous groups, and stakeholders to engage with policymakers. Examining the role of these groups in influencing global sustainability agendas underscores the importance of inclusive and participatory processes.

8. **Accountability and Reporting:** International agreements often include mechanisms for accountability and reporting on progress. Assessing the transparency and effectiveness of these mechanisms helps gauge the commitment of nations to their sustainability commitments.

9. **Barriers to Implementation:** Despite global commitments, there are often barriers to the implementation of sustainability goals. Identifying these barriers, such as financial constraints or political challenges, provides insights into the complexities of global sustainability efforts.

10. **Science and Technology:** Global agendas for sustainability also consider the role of science and technology in achieving environmental goals.

Analyzing discussions on innovation, research collaboration, and technology transfer reveals the potential for science to contribute to Earth protection.

11. **Funding and Support:** Adequate funding and support mechanisms are crucial for implementing sustainability agendas. Examining financial commitments, funding mechanisms, and international support for sustainable development projects highlights the resources dedicated to Earth protection.

12. **Interconnectedness of Goals:** Sustainability agendas recognize the interconnectedness of environmental, social, and economic goals. Analyzing how these goals are integrated and addressed collectively provides insights into holistic approaches to Earth protection.

By analyzing the outcomes and commitments from international forums and summits, we gain a deeper understanding of the priorities, challenges, and progress in global efforts to protect Earth. This examination helps assess the effectiveness of international cooperation in addressing environmental and sustainability challenges on a planetary scale.

Transnational Corporations and Environmental Responsibility:

Multinational corporations play a significant role in environmental impact. Investigating corporate environmental responsibility initiatives and their alignment with international goals contributes to understanding the private sector's role in Earth protection.

1. **Corporate Sustainability Strategies:** Many transnational corporations have adopted sustainability strategies that include environmental responsibility. Analyzing these strategies reveals how businesses integrate environmental concerns into their operations. This includes efforts to reduce carbon emissions, manage resources efficiently, and promote sustainable supply chains.

2. **Emissions Reduction Targets:** A key aspect of corporate environmental responsibility is setting emissions reduction targets. Examining the commitments made by multinational corporations to reduce their carbon footprint helps assess their contributions to global climate goals, such as those outlined in the Paris Agreement.

3. **Environmental Certifications and Standards:** Corporations often seek environmental certifications and adhere to international environmental standards. These certifications, such as ISO 14001 for environmental management, demonstrate a commitment to

environmentally sustainable practices. Evaluating the adoption and adherence to such standards provides insights into corporate environmental responsibility.

4. **Supply Chain Sustainability:** The supply chains of multinational corporations can have far-reaching environmental impacts. Analyzing efforts to promote sustainability throughout the supply chain, including responsible sourcing and ethical labor practices, demonstrates the broader approach to environmental responsibility.

5. **Investment in Renewable Energy:** Some corporations invest in renewable energy sources and technologies. Examining these investments highlights their contribution to clean energy production and the transition to a low-carbon economy.

6. **Circular Economy Initiatives:** A circular economy approach focuses on minimizing waste and maximizing resource efficiency. Investigating how multinational corporations embrace circular economy principles, such as recycling and waste reduction, provides insights into their efforts to reduce environmental harm.

7. **Environmental Reporting and Transparency:** Transparency is a crucial aspect of corporate environmental responsibility. Analyzing corporate environmental reporting practices, including the disclosure of environmental impact

assessments and sustainability reports, helps assess accountability and progress.

8. **Collaboration with NGOs and Stakeholders:** Some corporations collaborate with non-governmental organizations (NGOs) and stakeholders on environmental initiatives. Examining these partnerships reveals efforts to engage with civil society and address environmental challenges collectively.

9. **Corporate Social Responsibility (CSR):** Many corporations incorporate environmental responsibility into their broader corporate social responsibility initiatives. Evaluating CSR programs and their alignment with international environmental goals demonstrates the integration of sustainability into corporate values.

10. **Challenges and Criticisms:** Despite efforts, multinational corporations face challenges and criticisms regarding their environmental impact. Analyzing areas where corporations fall short or face controversies provides insights into the complexities of corporate environmental responsibility.

11. **Government Regulation and Compliance:** Multinational corporations operate in various countries with different regulatory frameworks. Assessing their compliance with environmental regulations and engagement with government

authorities helps gauge their commitment to legal and ethical standards.

12. **Environmental Innovation:** Some corporations invest in research and development for environmentally innovative technologies. Exploring these innovations sheds light on their potential to contribute to Earth protection and sustainable development.

By delving into the environmental responsibility initiatives of transnational corporations and their alignment with international goals, we can assess the extent to which the private sector is actively engaged in Earth protection. This examination also provides insights into the challenges and opportunities for corporations to contribute positively to global environmental efforts.

1. **Indigenous and Local Knowledge:**
Indigenous communities often possess valuable knowledge about sustainable land use and resource management. Examining efforts to incorporate indigenous and local knowledge into international conservation and protection strategies recognizes the importance of traditional wisdom.

1. **Traditional Ecological Knowledge (TEK):** Indigenous and local communities have developed Traditional Ecological Knowledge (TEK) over generations. This knowledge encompasses a deep understanding of local ecosystems, including plant and animal behavior, weather patterns, and sustainable land management practices. Analyzing how TEK is integrated into conservation and protection efforts highlights the potential for more holistic and sustainable approaches.

2. **Biodiversity Conservation:** Indigenous and local knowledge can significantly contribute to biodiversity conservation. Exploring how this knowledge is used to identify critical habitats, monitor wildlife populations, and protect endangered species offers insights into its role in international conservation strategies.

3. **Sustainable Resource Management:** Indigenous and local communities often have sustainable resource management practices that promote long-term ecological balance. Investigating how these practices are incorporated into international conservation and protection plans demonstrates their potential to address issues like deforestation, overfishing, and habitat degradation.

4. **Cultural Preservation:** The preservation of indigenous cultures is closely tied to environmental protection. Examining initiatives

that seek to safeguard both traditional knowledge and cultural practices underscores the interconnectedness of cultural and ecological diversity.

5. **Community-Led Conservation:** Some international conservation efforts prioritize community-led conservation models that empower indigenous and local communities to manage and protect their lands. Assessing the outcomes and challenges of such approaches sheds light on the effectiveness of community-based conservation.

6. **Legal Recognition:** International agreements, such as the Convention on Biological Diversity, recognize the significance of indigenous and local knowledge. Analyzing legal frameworks and policies that acknowledge and protect traditional knowledge reinforces its importance in global conservation efforts.

7. **Intellectual Property Rights:** Questions of intellectual property rights and benefit-sharing are crucial when incorporating indigenous knowledge into conservation strategies. Examining agreements that address these issues provides insights into efforts to ensure equitable sharing of benefits.

8. **Challenges and Barriers:** Incorporating indigenous and local knowledge into international conservation efforts is not without challenges.

Investigating the obstacles, including issues of cultural sensitivity, power dynamics, and language barriers, helps identify areas for improvement.

9. **Partnerships and Collaborations:** Partnerships between indigenous communities, governments, NGOs, and international organizations are instrumental in leveraging traditional knowledge for conservation. Analyzing successful collaborations highlights best practices in harnessing indigenous wisdom.

10. **Education and Capacity Building:** Efforts to build the capacity of indigenous and local communities in conservation and protection practices are essential. Exploring educational programs and training initiatives demonstrates a commitment to empowering communities to be stewards of their environments.

11. **Sustainability and Resilience:** Indigenous and local knowledge often emphasizes sustainability and resilience in the face of environmental changes. Assessing how these principles are integrated into international strategies can provide valuable lessons for adapting to a changing world.

12. **Cultural and Ethical Considerations:** Recognizing the cultural and ethical dimensions of incorporating indigenous knowledge is vital. Examining how respect for cultural values and

ethical principles guides conservation efforts ensures a balanced approach.

By delving into the incorporation of indigenous and local knowledge into international conservation and protection strategies, we can acknowledge the invaluable contributions of these communities to Earth protection. This exploration also highlights the need for respectful partnerships and policies that recognize and preserve traditional wisdom in the pursuit of sustainable environmental practices.

Environmental Justice Movements:

Grassroots environmental justice movements advocate for Earth protection. Analyzing the impact and influence of such movements on international agendas and policies highlights the role of civil society in global environmental efforts.

1. **Origins and Objectives:** Understanding the origins and objectives of environmental justice movements provides context for their advocacy. These movements often emerge in response to environmental injustices, such as pollution in marginalized communities or threats to sacred natural sites.

2. **Community-Based Advocacy:** Environmental justice movements are often rooted in affected

communities. Examining how these movements empower local communities to address environmental concerns sheds light on their grassroots nature and their focus on localized issues.

3. **Environmental Racism:** Many environmental justice movements highlight issues of environmental racism, where vulnerable and marginalized communities face disproportionate environmental harms. Analyzing cases of environmental racism and the responses of these movements helps expose systemic injustices.

4. **Policy Advocacy:** These movements engage in policy advocacy at various levels of government, from local ordinances to international agreements. Investigating their influence on policy decisions and environmental regulations provides insights into their effectiveness.

5. **Direct Action and Protest:** Environmental justice movements may resort to direct action and protest to draw attention to pressing issues. Examining the impact of such actions on public awareness and policy change underscores their role in advocacy.

6. **Intersectionality:** Environmental justice movements often recognize the intersectionality of social and environmental issues. Exploring how they address issues like gender equality, Indigenous rights, and economic justice within

their advocacy broadens our understanding of their scope.

7. **International Solidarity:** Some environmental justice movements form alliances with similar groups globally. Analyzing international solidarity efforts and their impact on transnational environmental advocacy illustrates the interconnectedness of environmental justice struggles.

8. **Legal Strategies:** Environmental justice movements may pursue legal strategies, including lawsuits against polluters or demands for reparations. Assessing the outcomes of legal actions taken by these movements demonstrates their commitment to accountability.

9. **Media and Communication:** These movements use media and communication channels to amplify their messages. Investigating their media strategies and their ability to shape public discourse provides insights into their influence.

10. **Impact on International Agendas:** Analyzing how environmental justice movements have influenced international environmental agendas, such as discussions on climate change and biodiversity, showcases their role in shaping global priorities.

11. **Barriers and Challenges:** Environmental justice movements often face challenges, including

repression and lack of resources. Examining the obstacles they encounter in their advocacy efforts highlights the resilience and determination of these movements.

12. **Future Directions:** Exploring the future directions of environmental justice movements, including their evolving strategies and goals, can provide a glimpse into the continued importance of their work in Earth protection.

By delving into the impact and influence of environmental justice movements on international agendas and policies, we gain a deeper appreciation of the critical role civil society plays in advocating for environmental protection and justice. These movements serve as powerful agents of change, pushing for policies and practices that prioritize both environmental sustainability and social equity.

In conclusion, an analysis of international efforts to protect Earth involves examining a complex web of agreements, organizations, scientific collaborations, and ethical considerations. Understanding the strategies and challenges faced by world leaders, both in the public and private sectors, in safeguarding the environment is crucial for evaluating the collective commitment to Earth protection on a global scale.

Chapter 13: Conclusion

In this final chapter, we bring together the key points from each chapter of our book, "Stop Destroying Earth: A Wake-Up Call to Safeguard Our Planet's Future," and emphasize the urgent need for change.

1. **Biodiversity and Extinction:** We began by delving into the Extinction Crisis, highlighting the grave threats posed by habitat destruction, climate change, poaching, pollution, and invasive species. Our exploration underscored the urgency of preserving Earth's biodiversity.

2. **Population Reduction Strategies:** We examined expectations for reducing population growth through strategies such as family planning, empowering women, voluntary measures, education, access to healthcare, delayed parenthood, and urbanization.

3. **Pandemics and the Future:** In this chapter, we explored the potential impact of future viruses, considering factors like transmission dynamics, healthcare infrastructure, and global interconnectedness.

4. **The Specter of War:** We discussed the possibility of future large-scale conflicts, analyzing evolving

conflict landscapes, resource scarcity, geopolitical rivalries, proxy wars, and cyber threats.

5. **Protecting Earth:** Our examination of international efforts, including Sustainable Development Goals, climate change agreements, biodiversity conservation conventions, and the roles of organizations, provided insights into safeguarding Earth.

6. **Global Perspectives:** We emphasized the importance of a global perspective, analyzing urbanization trends, resource competition, geopolitical rivalries, and the role of international organizations in shaping Earth's future.

7. **Ethical Considerations:** Throughout our exploration, we continuously discussed ethical dimensions, including individual rights, equity, and environmental justice, highlighting the moral imperative of Earth protection.

8. **Conclusion:** In this concluding chapter, we reiterate the urgency of the environmental challenges we face. Our book serves as a comprehensive wake-up call, revealing the interconnectedness of these issues and the need for collective action.

Our planet's future hangs in the balance, and the destructive behaviors that have brought us to this critical juncture must change. As we summarize the wealth of information presented in this book, we emphasize the importance of individual and collective responsibility. Earth is our shared home, and safeguarding its future requires immediate action.

This book aims to inspire readers to take proactive steps, both in their personal lives and as advocates for change. We believe that by raising awareness, fostering a deeper understanding of these issues, and emphasizing the interconnectedness of our world, we can chart a path toward a more sustainable and harmonious future for Earth and all its inhabitants. The time to act is now, and together, we can make a difference.

About Author

Osman Karakas is an accomplished journalist, editor, researcher, photographer, and author with a diverse and extensive background in the field of journalism. With a passion for storytelling and a commitment to journalistic integrity, Osman Karakas has made significant contributions to the media industry throughout his career.

Osman Karakas has been recognized for his outstanding work and has received numerous awards and accolades. In 1991, he was honored with the Excellence in Journalism award by the Deadline Club-Society of Professional Journalists in New York, USA.

In 1990, Osman Karakas won first place in the Spot News category at the Associated Press Association, New York, for his impactful news story titled "Don't Let Him Die" published in the New York Post.

He also received the prestigious Picture of the Year Award in 1990 from the University of Missouri - School of Journalism/National Press Photographers Association, his photography was compared to Michelangelo's "Pieta" by the head of the jury.

His international experience continued as they worked as a correspondent at the United Nations for Anadolu Weekly in New York, USA, and later as a Correspondent and News & Photo Editor for Hurriyet International Daily, covering press conferences at the UN.

In addition to his international assignments, Osman Karakas his career in journalism as a correspondent for TRT (Turkish Radio & Television) in Turkmenistan and Kazakhstan from 1993 to 1996. During this time, they also served as the Editor-in-Chief of the TURKCAN International Magazine in Turkmenistan. Also manager and editor-in-Chief various newspapers and magazines in Türkiye and Central Asia.

Osman Karakas has been involved in academia as well, having worked as a Lecturer at Manas University in Bishkek, Kyrgyzstan, where they taught journalism courses, advised students, and served on various committees about 8 years. His dedication to education and knowledge sharing has been instrumental in nurturing the next generation of journalists.

With proficiency in multiple languages, including English, Turkish, Russian, Turkmen, Azerbaijan, Kyrgyz, and Kazakh, Osman Karakas has been able to communicate and report on diverse topics with cultural sensitivity and understanding. his language skills have allowed them to engage with various communities and provide insightful coverage.

Alongside his journalistic career, Osman Karakas has authored several books and documentaries, covering topics ranging from journalism to detective novels and documentaries on historical events. They have also exhibited his photography in multiple personal exhibitions in Turkey and Kyrgyzstan, showcasing his artistic talent and unique perspective.

Osman Karakas possesses a wide range of skills and expertise, including diplomacy, media relations, public relations, political campaign management, managing media, photography, communication, and web publishing. Including; advertising, social media, and desktop publishing, keeping up with the evolving landscape of digital journalism.

In conclusion, Osman Karakas has made significant contributions to the field of journalism through his exceptional work, awards, publications, and dedication to journalistic ethics. His diverse experiences, international exposure, and commitment to storytelling have shaped his career and established them as a respected figure in the media industry.

Recommended Books

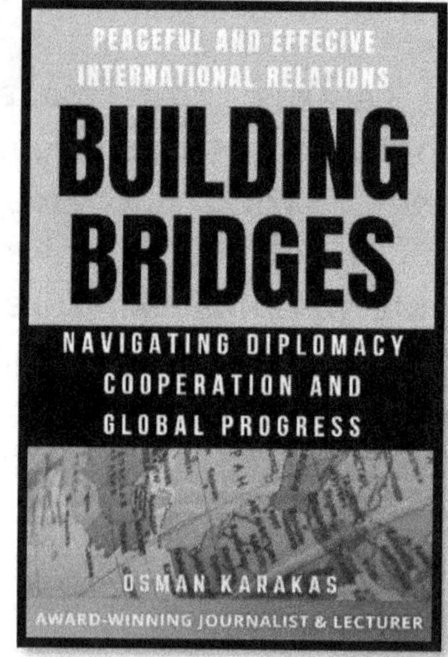

COMPREHENSIVE GUIDE THAT EXPLORES THE
INTRICATE WORLD OF CRISIS DIPLOMACY
ART OF
DIPLOMACY
IN CRISES
NAVIGATING INTERNATIONAL
RELATIONS WITH FINESSE AND
STRATEGIC EXCELLENCE
OSMAN KARAKAS

THE SOCIAL
MEDIA
PARADOX
Citizen Journalism or
Social Media Terror?
OSMAN KARAKAS
AWARD-WINNING JOURNALIST & LECTURER

INTERNATIONAL
JOURNALISM
Global Perspectives of
International News
OSMAN KARAKAS
AWARD-WINNING JOURNALIST & LECTURER

Journalists
Selling Their Pen in
the Media World
EMBEDDED
/JERKS
OSMAN KARAKAS
AWARD-WINNING JOURNALIST & LECTURER

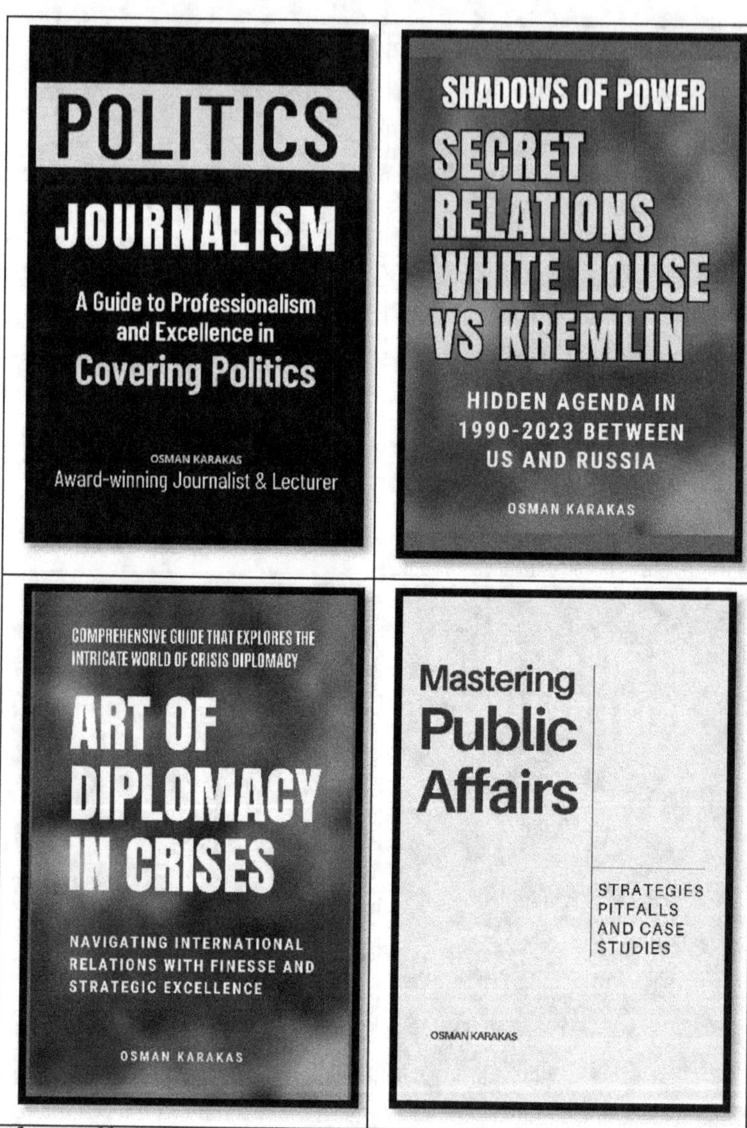

The collection of books is accessible for purchase on Amazon.com platform.